PTSD

Proven Psychological Techniques for Managing

(The Psychology of Post-traumatic Stress Disorder and the Ethical Way)

Andres James

Published By **Bengion Cosalas**

Andres James

All Rights Reserved

*Ptsd: Proven Psychological Techniques for
Managing (The Psychology of Post-traumatic
Stress Disorder and the Ethical Way)*

ISBN   978-1-7771996-7-8

Legal & Disclaimer

Table Of Contents

Chapter 1: Understanding What Ptsd Is ... 1

Chapter 2: Myths And Facts About Post Traumatic Stress Disorder (Ptsd).............. 9

Chapter 3: Tips To Help Cope With Ptsd 21

Chapter 4: Complementary & Alternative (Cam) Treatment For Ptsd...................... 51

Chapter 5: Ptsd & Diet 62

Chapter 6: What Is Emotional Trauma ... 73

Chapter 7: How To Recover From Emotional Trauma; 91

Chapter 8: Break The Bonds Of The Past 122

Chapter 9: Definition Of Ptsd 132

Chapter 10: Causes And Risk Factors ... 143

Chapter 11: Medications...................... 158

Chapter 12: Mindfulness And Meditation 173

Chapter 1: Understanding What Ptsd Is

Post-worrying strain sickness (PTSD) is a highbrow fitness condition that could rise up after a annoying experience. It produces ugly, anxious feelings. Some folks with PTSD take into account the incident all once more and over. Others shun any reminders of it. PTSD interferes with life, technique and relationships. Yet, medicinal drug and treatment may also moreover moreover assist, even years afterwards.

WHAT IS POST-TRAUMATIC STRESS DISORDER?

Post-disturbing pressure infection (PTSD) is a highbrow health scenario which could growth after a daunting experience. The prevalence may be lethal, life-threatening, horrifying or mainly terrifying. Examples embody:

Accident.

Fire.

Military struggle.

Natural calamities, along with a tornado.

Physical abuse.

Sexual assault or rape.

The unexpected demise of a cherished one.

Terrorist assault.

The terrible incident may additionally have happened to you, or you could have watched it occur to someone else.

It's less high-priced to experience sad after something like that takes region. You may additionally have troubles sound asleep, ingesting or doing sports you need for a quick length. Yet with PTSD, signs and symptoms and signs and symptoms undergo longer than some months and intervene alongside aspect your lifestyles.

HOW COMMON IS PTSD?

At least half the population within the United States have suffered a stressful incident. In this population, 10% of guys and 20% of girls be afflicted via way of PTSD. Women face forget about or abuse within the course of teenagers greater normally than guys. Girls moreover endure sexual assault and home abuse greater regularly. Women commonly generally have a tendency to revel in trauma in a completely unique way than males, too.

ARE SOME PEOPLE MORE LIKELY TO DEVELOP PTSD THAN OTHERS?

There's no way to count on who may additionally moreover gather PTSD following a excessive incident. Yet, PTSD is more likely amongst humans who've experienced:

Some types of trauma, encompass navy warfare or sexual abuse.

Injuries at some point of the healthy.

Absence of help from loved ones following a horrible prevalence.

Long-lasting or repetitive trauma.

Personal information of tension or melancholy, even in advance than the stressful experience.

Intense instant reaction to the incident (for instance, shaking or vomiting up).

Extremely robust trauma.

SYMPTOMS AND CAUSES

What Causes PTSD?

A demanding revel in creates PTSD. Nevertheless, professionals aren't clean why some people have PTSD and others don't.

WHAT ARE THE SYMPTOMS OF PTSD?

PTSD signs and symptoms and symptoms variety from character to character. Nonetheless, all people with PTSD suffers one or greater of the subsequent:

AVOIDING THINGS:

You may additionally avoid humans or situations that remind you of the superiority. Examples encompass pals you met within the army provider, the phase of metropolis where you encountered the trauma or crowds in fashionable. Some oldsters with PTSD try to keep so busy that they don't reflect onconsideration on the incident.

BEING ON EDGE:

The infection may make it hard as a way to loosen up or enjoy the property you used to. You may additionally additionally furthermore enjoy agitated or stressful. Maybe you're resultseasily greatly surprised or constantly anticipate some component horrible to appear. You also might also moreover have problems slumbering or focusing.

HAVING NEGATIVE THOUGHTS AND FEELINGS:

PTSD also can moreover make you enjoy lousy, angry, depressed, mistrustful, responsible, or numb.

RELIVING OR RE-EXPERIENCING THE TRAUMATIC EVENT:

This may moreover take the form of flashbacks or nightmares. Sometimes a noise like a vehicle backfiring or witnessing a few detail similar (for instance, a hearth) can elicit abrupt, unwanted memories.

HOW DOES PTSD AFFECT YOUR LIFE?

PTSD may additionally furthermore reason various problems together together with your fitness and lifestyles, which includes:

Alcohol and drug usage.

Anxiety.

Depression.

Thoughts of hurting your self or others.

Difficulties at artwork and on your non-public connections.

Children With PTSD May :

Act out the disturbing event on the equal time as gambling.

Cling to a figure or different grownup.

Forget a way to speak, or at the least faux to.

Wet the bed no matter the reality that they comprehend a manner to apply the relaxation room.

DIAGNOSIS AND TESTS

How is PTSD recognized?

There's no take a look at or blood test for PTSD. If you've encountered a traumatic incident and are displaying signs and symptoms of PTSD, communicate to a healthcare expert.

The healthcare expert could likely determine the analysis based totally totally mostly on a communicate approximately your signs and signs. To be labelled PTSD, symptoms and signs need to go through longer than a month and interfere collectively together with your existence.

MANAGEMENT AND TREATMENT

The extremely good remedy for PTSD includes remedy and trauma-targeted counselling.

Certain tablets may additionally additionally furthermore help your body create greater chemical substances that control pressure and feelings. They come into   important lessons:

Selective Serotonin Reuptake Inhibitors (occasionally termed SSRIs).

Serotonin-norepinephrine Reuptake Inhibitors (additionally referred to as SNRIs).

Trauma-centered treatment research the incident and its implications. It may be done in some of precise strategies:

COGNITIVE PROCESSING THERAPY:

This treatment analyzes awful thoughts and ideals about the demanding incident and seeks to alter them.

EYE MOVEMENT DESENSITIZATION AND REPROCESSING (EMDR):

Chapter 2: Myths And Facts About Post Traumatic Stress Disorder (Ptsd)

MYTH: PTSD is simplest because of military fight.

FACT: PTSD can be as a consequence of any demanding occasion, at the side of sexual assault, herbal failures, automobile accidents, or witnessing violence.

MYTH: Only vulnerable human beings get PTSD.

FACT: PTSD can show as much as surely everybody who reviews a disturbing event, no matter their power or resilience.

MYTH: Everyone who tales a stressful occasion will increase PTSD.

FACT: While many people who experience trauma can also additionally have transient symptoms, no longer every body will increase PTSD.

MYTH: PTSD is a sign of weak point.

FACT: PTSD is a intellectual health situation due to trauma, now not a sign of weakness.

MYTH: Only veterans can get PTSD.

FACT: Anyone who has professional a traumatic event can increase PTSD, collectively with civilians, emergency responders, and patients of crime.

MYTH: PTSD is uncommon.

FACT: PTSD is clearly quite not unusual, affecting an predicted 7-8% of the population in some unspecified time within the destiny in their lives.

MYTH: PTSD satisfactory influences adults.

FACT: Children can also amplify PTSD after experiencing a demanding occasion.

MYTH: If you have PTSD, it method you're crazy.

FACT: PTSD is a treatable intellectual fitness situation, and having it does not recommend a person is crazy.

MYTH: People with PTSD will never simply get better.

FACT: With suitable treatment and guide, many people with PTSD can definitely recover.

MYTH: PTSD notable affects your intellectual fitness.

FACT: PTSD also can have bodily signs, together with complications, belly troubles, and sleep disturbances.

MYTH: PTSD is continuously because of a single demanding event.

FACT: PTSD also can be due to repeated or ongoing trauma, consisting of home abuse or youth overlook.

MYTH: People with PTSD are violent.

FACT: People with PTSD are not any more likely to be violent than people with out the situation.

MYTH: PTSD fine impacts individuals who are without delay concerned in a stressful event.

FACT: PTSD can also have an effect on individuals who witness a worrying occasion, collectively with a bystander to a violent crime.

MYTH: PTSD is a today's situation.

FACT: PTSD has been recognized as a highbrow fitness scenario since the Eighties, but the symptoms and signs and symptoms and signs have been documented in some unspecified time in the destiny of information below one among a kind names.

MYTH: PTSD only affects folks who are emotionally touchy.

FACT: PTSD can affect every body, no matter their emotional sensitivity.

MYTH: PTSD constantly consists of flashbacks.

FACT: While flashbacks are a common symptom of PTSD, no longer every body with the situation critiques them.

MYTH: People with PTSD are susceptible-willed.

FACT: PTSD is due to trauma, no longer weak point of person.

MYTH: PTSD can be cured with medicine by myself.

FACT: While treatment can be beneficial for coping with some symptoms of PTSD, it is also handiest even as utilized in mixture with treatment.

MYTH: Only humans with intense trauma can develop PTSD.

FACT: PTSD can growth after any annoying event, regardless of its severity.

MYTH: People with PTSD are just on the lookout for interest.

FACT: PTSD is a severe intellectual health situation that may have a massive effect on someone's life, and people with the scenario aren't trying to find interest.

MYTH: PTSD excellent affects mother and father that are bodily injured.

FACT: PTSD can expand after any annoying occasion, whether or now not bodily harm is concerned.

MYTH: PTSD is straightforward to diagnose.

FACT: Diagnosing PTSD may be tough, as signs and symptoms and symptoms can overlap with other highbrow health situations.

MYTH: PTSD first-rate affects parents which can be inclined-minded.

FACT: PTSD is due to trauma, now not vulnerable point of mind.

MYTH: PTSD generally consists of nightmares.

FACT: While nightmares are a common symptom of PTSD, now not truely every body with the situation memories them.

MYTH: PTSD is a sign of mental contamination.

FACT: PTSD is a intellectual fitness scenario, but it does now not imply someone is mentally unwell. It is a normal response to an atypical situation.

MYTH: If you've got PTSD, you can constantly have it.

FACT: With remedy, many people with PTSD can get higher and lead wholesome, pleasing lives.

MYTH: PTSD isn't always treatable.

FACT: PTSD is treatable with severa treatments, together with cognitive-behavioral remedy, eye movement desensitization and reprocessing (EMDR), and medicine.

MYTH: PTSD treatment is too costly.

FACT: Many groups provide unfastened or low-charge PTSD remedy for veterans, and a few insurance plans cover PTSD remedy.

MYTH: People with PTSD are violent and perilous.

FACT: People with PTSD are not any more violent or unstable than all people else. In fact, they're more likely to damage themselves than others.

MYTH: People with PTSD cannot feature in normal existence.

FACT: While PTSD may be debilitating, many human beings with PTSD are capable of characteristic in normal life with treatment and assist.

MYTH: PTSD most effective impacts the person that skilled the trauma.

FACT: PTSD also can have an impact at the individual's own family, friends, and coworkers, as they will revel in secondary trauma or have to cope with the person's symptoms.

MYTH: Only people who've skilled a single demanding occasion can amplify PTSD.

FACT: People who have professional repeated trauma, which encompass abuse or fight, also are at danger for developing PTSD.

MYTH: If someone has not advanced PTSD immediately after a annoying event, they by no means will.

FACT: Symptoms of PTSD can amplify months or possibly years after a worrying event.

MYTH: People with PTSD want to avoid speaking approximately the trauma.

FACT: Talking approximately the trauma in a safe and supportive surroundings may be a part of the healing method for human beings with PTSD.

MYTH: PTSD is due to a weak factor in the character's persona.

FACT: PTSD is not due to individual flaws, but alternatively by way of manner of exposure to trauma.

MYTH: PTSD is a form of hysteria disorder.

FACT: While PTSD does include tension signs and symptoms, it's far a separate and first rate illness.

MYTH: PTSD isn't always a intense condition.

FACT: PTSD is a severe state of affairs that can have a massive impact on someone's lifestyles, relationships, and easy well-being.

MYTH: PTSD is a new situation.

FACT: PTSD has been recognized as a highbrow health scenario because the Nineteen Eighties, however it's been defined under certainly one of a type names for the duration of history.

In conclusion, publish-traumatic strain illness (PTSD) is a complicated intellectual health situation that might have an impact on people who've experienced or witnessed a worrying event. Although there are various myths and misconceptions surrounding PTSD, it is crucial to recognize the statistics in case you need to provide proper beneficial resource and remedy for the ones affected.

One of the largest myths approximately PTSD is that it simplest influences veterans or humans in immoderate-risk professions. However, PTSD will have an effect on every person who has professional or witnessed a traumatic event, which include sexual attack, a vehicle twist of future, or a natural disaster. Another commonplace misconception is that people with PTSD are vulnerable or someway at fault for their signs and symptoms and signs. In fact, PTSD is a critical scientific state of affairs that calls for professional remedy and help.

Effective treatments for PTSD include treatment, treatment, and self-care techniques which encompass exercise and mindfulness practices. It is important for individuals with PTSD to are looking for assist from licensed intellectual fitness specialists and to surround themselves with a supportive network of friends and own family.

While there can be regardless of the truth that a whole lot to discover about PTSD, debunking myths and knowledge the facts is a crucial step in reducing the stigma and improving effects for human beings with this example. By spotting the fact of PTSD and offering appropriate resource, we are able to help the ones affected to heal and thrive.

Chapter 3: Tips To Help Cope With Ptsd

SELF-HELP TIPS FOR COPING WITH PTSD

Self-assist measures, like meditating, taking part in exercising, finding social manual, and using aromatherapy is probably powerful for controlling PTSD signs and symptoms at home.

Post-worrying strain illness (PTSD) is a situation that produces flashbacks, nightmares and unpleasant signs and symptoms and signs which includes rage, sleep issues and a horrible perspective of the place, following struggling a risky or terrifying incident such as sexual assault or a existence-threatening twist of destiny. Although there may be remedy available for PTSD, some people must discover ways to deal with PTSD triggers on their very private with the resource of utilizing self-assist processes. These 8 strategies also can help you manage with PTSD.

MEDITATE

Through meditation, you could discover ways to be greater alert and privy to the current 2nd. While running toward mindfulness, you can turn out to be extra aware of physiological sensations, mind and feelings and discover PTSD triggers. Meditation can also moreover assist humans with PTSD to conquer unwanted thoughts and memories and allow them to skip without judgment.

Studies show that meditation for PTSD is powerful. A check of 10 separate trials reveals that contemplative sports activities help alleviate PTSD signs. Guided meditation, this is taught with the resource of a certified practitioner, may be very useful for individuals recovery from PTSD.

One research including a guided meditation for PTSD indicated that once veterans with this disorder attended weekly meditation commands for four weeks, they saw sizeable decreases within the strain hormone cortisol. The meditation exercise become established to be greater useful than preferred PTSD treatment.

STAY ACTIVE

PTSD with exercising can be a effective mixture while you take into account that workout enhances mood and can assist with PTSD signs and symptoms like tension and irritability. Physical workout can also be a deliver of entertainment and bring respite from flashbacks and lousy perceptions of the area. Individuals may additionally additionally find out that bodily interest gives social beneficial aid inside the occasion that they need to join a walking membership or attend group workout instructions at a gym or health center.

Workout remedy plans were validated to be beneficial for people residing with PTSD. A new assessment of the proof famous that exercise improves PTSD signs and symptoms and signs and symptoms and disappointment. It is also highlighted that PTSD is related to fitness concerns like coronary heart sickness, therefore bodily exercising is extraordinary for people with this intellectual health situation.

GET A SERVICE DOG

PTSD company dogs may additionally moreover deliver enterprise and a relaxing effect for people with PTSD. Organizations consisting of Service Dogs for America supply records on the manner to acquire a carrier canine for PTSD. Service puppies for America welcomes packages for carrier puppies and could get hold of them from people with PTSD, irrespective of whether they'll be participants of the military. This organisation trains dogs to cope with the necessities of oldsters with PTSD.

For example, the puppies learn how to pick out the symptoms of PTSD which incorporates anxiety and nightmares and to intervene when these symptoms and symptoms and symptoms get up.

PTSD issuer puppies can also deliver manual and useful resource in severa ways. Cats might also inspire someone to wake from a nightmare or bring consolation at some stage in instances of distress thru pawing at or prodding their proprietors. They may also moreover moreover provide diversions, supply treatment to a person, or inform others that useful useful resource is needed at some point of disaster sports.

SET BOUNDARIES

Family and buddies can be touched thru using a unmarried man or woman's struggling with PTSD. Relationships may be a trouble for people with PTSD and their cherished ones. It is vital to create limitations in any dating, specifically whilst PTSD or other ailments are present.

When someone is subjected to a traumatic revel in which includes sexual attack or a natural disaster, their boundaries and feeling of protection are broken. In interactions with friends, circle of relatives or a vast one in every of a kind, it's miles for that reason crucial to cope with PTSD triggers and encourage cherished ones to surely receive while location or time by myself is needed.

Individuals in healing from PTSD say that growing boundaries and maintaining private region is useful for reducing anxiety. When a cherished one is overbearing or limits private vicinity to someone with PTSD, the person with PTSD may also feel uncomfortable. To boost feelings of safety, it's miles essential to have a communicate with family and pals approximately limits and the way they'll recognize them.

If someone has crossed a boundary or invaded personal location, taking a step away or asking them to transport again or lower their voice is beneficial. Occasionally, it can be critical to walk a ways from a state of affairs if obstacles had been damaged.

FIND A CREATIVE OUTLET

Artistic sports activities which include artwork therapy for PTSD and track treatment for PTSD may additionally moreover have a first rate have an impact on on signs and signs and symptoms and symptoms. Other sports activities on the aspect of creative writing or handicraft would possibly bring respite from tension and anger. Some professionals suppose that revolutionary hobbies like quilting or paintings responsibilities may be correct for folks that don't get the respite they want from ordinary psychiatric remedy.

Thankfully, evidence suggests that revolutionary treatment can be useful for PTSD. In a studies with veterans, a song intervention modified into shown to dramatically decrease signs of disappointment and the severity of PTSD.

Additional Artistic Interests For Veterans With PTSD Could Include:

Woodworking

Learning to play an device

Painting

Singing in a choir

Cooking

Journaling

Sewing

CREATE A SUPPORT NETWORK

Having a PTSD assist community also can be top for managing this highbrow fitness hassle. Having friends, own family members, or a colleague who is aware of approximately your PTSD and is out there to talk approximately might be critical for rehabilitation. A PTSD community is probably there to pay attention and deliver answers at some point of hard instances.

Social help has been showed to be especially critical for people who've been uncovered to repeated traumatic situations. One studies indicated that the opportunity of PTSD become 17 times massive in girls who were exposed to every little one abuse and rape, no matter the truth that the degree of PTSD have come to be decrease in people who acquired extra social help. Social assist can also therefore reduce a number of the symptoms and symptoms and signs and symptoms related with trauma.

TRY AROMATHERAPY

Aromatherapy, it really is the approach of the use of vital oils to treatment illnesses starting from headache to melancholy, also can entail diffusing, inhalation, inner absorption or utilizing oils at the pores and pores and pores and skin. Aromatherapy for PTSD might also furthermore encompass crucial oils which includes rose, lavender, ylang-ylang, sage and chamomile, which may be recognized for his or her enjoyable outcomes.

Aromatherapy is known to have a relaxing impact, therefore it is probably powerful for treating PTSD signs and symptoms and symptoms like tension and agitation. A evaluation of facts suggests that aromatherapy is frequently useful for reducing tension. In addition, essential oils could likely ease sleep disruptions in patients with PTSD, as one research determined out that lavender oil superior sleep exceptional extra than merely education healthful sleep practices.

SEEK COUNSELING

Although self-help strategies may be powerful for handling PTSD, some human beings also can find out that they require greater remedy inside the form of counseling. According to the National Alliance on Mental Illness (NAMI), PTSD treatment can also additionally moreover contain the subsequent counseling styles:

COGNITIVE PROCESSING THERAPY – This fashion of counseling has origins in cognitive behavioural remedy and allows individuals with PTSD to research to triumph over terrible thoughts and feelings of self-blame.

EYE MOVEMENT DESENSITIZATION AND REPROCESSING (EMDR) – Developed expressly to cope with trauma, EMDR remedy exposes a person to memories of a worrying incident while moreover moving the eyes to test other stimuli.

EXPOSURE THERAPY – In exposure remedy, a professional practitioner allows a client assemble methods for handling trauma through exposing them to triggers, often thru digital truth.

GROUP THERAPY – In this form of remedy, people with PTSD get aid from and analyze coping techniques from others who are experiencing similar signs and symptoms.

Seeking out the shape of varieties of PTSD treatment from a professional therapist can also moreover moreover lessen signs and symptoms and assist patients discover techniques to control PTSD

SUPPORTING SOMEONE WITH PTSD

When someone you care about suffers from post-stressful stress ailment, it may be demanding. Yet with the ones actions, you could help your beloved skip on with their life.

Women sharing ache, embracing

LIVING WITH SOMEONE WHO HAS PTSD

When a partner, buddy, or member of the family suffers put up-traumatic strain illness (PTSD) it affects you, too. PTSD isn't clean to live with and it could take a big toll on relationships and own family existence. You may be wounded with the aid of the one that you love's remoteness and moodiness or straining to comprehend their behaviour—why they will be much much less loving and extra risky. You may additionally experience which consist of you're taking walks on eggshells or dwelling with a stranger.

You also can have to take in a better proportion of domestic responsibilities and cope with the frustration of a cherished one that received't open up. The signs and symptoms and signs and signs and symptoms of PTSD may additionally even bring about job loss, drug misuse, and first rate issues that effect the complete circle of relatives.

It's tough no longer to take the symptoms of PTSD for my part, but it's essential to recognize that someone with PTSD may not continually have manipulate over their behavior.

Your cherished one's disturbing gadget is "caught" in a rustic of perpetual alert, making them time and again enjoy inclined and perilous, or having to relive the terrible incident yet again and over. This also can reason anger, impatience, despair, mistrust, and unique PTSD symptoms that the one you love can't definitely pick out out to show off.

With the right help from you and different family and pals, but, the one that you love's worried device may also moreover furthermore get "unstuck." With these recommendations, you can assist them to in the long run pass on from the terrible experience and allow your lifestyles together to go lower lower back to regular.

HELPING SOMEONE WITH PTSD TIP 1: PROVIDE SOCIAL SUPPORT

It's ordinary for people with PTSD to withdraw from family and pals. They may additionally sense humiliated, no longer want to burden others or expect that other people won't understand what they're going thru. Although it's important to recognize the only that you love's limits, your comfort and useful resource may moreover help them overcome emotions of helplessness, loss, and despair. In reality, trauma experts experience that face-to-face help from others is the most important component in PTSD rehabilitation.

Understanding a manner to efficiently display your love and help for a person with PTSD is not easy. You can't strain the one that you love to get properly, however you could play a massive component inside the restoration method via simply spending time with them.

DON'T PUSH YOUR LOVED ONE INTO TALKING.

It can be quite tough for people with PTSD to talk approximately their terrible stories. For others, it might even reason them to experience worse. Instead, allow them to recognise you're organized to concentrate once they want to talk, or without a doubt loaf around when they do not. Comfort for a person with PTSD comes from feeling concerned and commonplace via manner of you, not constantly from chatting.

DO "NORMAL" ACTIVITIES WITH YOUR LOVED ONE, THINGS THAT HAVE NOTHING TO DO WITH PTSD OR THE TERRIBLE INCIDENT.

Urge the one that you love to are looking for companions, discover sports that provide them pleasure, and have interaction in a rhythmic sports which encompass taking walks, walking, swimming, or rock climbing. Join a fitness elegance collectively, pass dancing, or set up a normal lunch appointment with pals and family.

LET YOUR LOVED ONE TAKE THE LEAD, RATHER THAN INSTRUCTING THEM WHAT TO DO.

Everyone with PTSD is one-of-a-kind however maximum people intuitively apprehend what allows them experience non violent and cushty. Take clues from the only that you love as to how you'll likely incredible supply help and agency.

HANDLE YOUR OWN STRESS. The extra calm, peaceful, and concentrated you are, the more you will be capable of useful useful aid the one that you love.

BE PATIENT. Recovery is a way that takes time and often consists of setbacks. The critical detail is to hold thrilled and preserve to guide the one which you love.

INFORM YOURSELF ABOUT PTSD.

The more about the signs and symptoms, consequences, and treatment picks, the better organized you'll be to useful useful resource the one you love, recognize what they are going thru, and hold topics in mindset.

ACCEPT (AND ANTICIPATE) MIXED SENTIMENTS.

When you go through the emotional wringer, be prepared for a complicated mixture of feelings—some of which you may in no way need to simply accept. Just preserve in thoughts, having unfavorable thoughts about your family member may want to no longer advocate you don't love them.

TIP 2: BE A GOOD LISTENER

Although you should not encourage someone with PTSD to talk if they do want to proportion, try to pay attention without expectations or selections. Make it apparent that you're worried and which you care, however don't stress about delivering advice. It's the act of listening carefully this is beneficial to the most effective that you love, no longer what you assert.

A man or woman with PTSD might also moreover want to talk about the painful incident time and again all once more. This is a part of the restoration approach, so resist the selection to signify the one that you love to prevent reliving the beyond and skip on. Instead, provide to speak as frequently as they want.

Some of the subjects the one which you love says may be quite hard to pay attention to. It's adequate to detest what you pay interest, however it's vital to recognize their sentiments and responses. If you come across as disapproving, terrified, or essential, they're not possibly to divulge heart's contents to you again.

Communication Pitfalls To Avoid

Don't:

Offer smooth answers or carelessly assure the one you love the whole lot is going to be all right.

Stop the one that you love from speakme approximately their feelings or anxieties.

Give unsolicited advice or inform the one you love what they "ought to" do.

Blame all of your relationship or circle of relatives troubles on the one that you love's PTSD.

Invalidate, reduce, or reject the one that you love's horrible revel in

Issue ultimatums or make threats or desires.

Make your loved one feel prone for the reason that they may be no longer dealing in addition to others.

Remind the one that you love they had been lucky it wasn't worse.

Take over together along with your non-public critiques or sentiments.

TIP 3: REBUILD TRUST AND SAFETY

Trauma transforms the manner a person perceives the world, making it appear to be a constantly volatile and terrifying vicinity. It moreover impairs human beings's potential to keep in mind others and themselves. If there may be any manner you could recreate your loved one's feeling of safety, it will help their rehabilitation.

COMMUNICATE YOUR DEDICATION TO THE PARTNERSHIP.

Let your loved one apprehend that you're here for the lengthy haul truely so that they revel in cherished and supported.

DEVELOP ROUTINES

Structure and constant bodily games assist provide a feel of stability and comfort to humans with PTSD, which includes adults and kids. Establishing physical sports may additionally suggest asking your beloved to help with shopping for or residence duties, for instance, retaining regular times for food, or actually "being there" for the man or woman.

REDUCE STRESS AT HOME.

Strive to make certain the one you love receives vicinity and time for rest and relaxation.

TALK ABOUT THE FUTURE AND ESTABLISH PREPARATIONS.

This may also assist combat the normal sensation among people with PTSD that their destiny is restrained.

KEEP YOUR COMMITMENTS.

Help reestablish consider via proving that you're honest. Be normal and observe via on what you claim you may do.

HIGHLIGHT YOUR LOVED ONE'S STRENGTHS.

Inform your beloved you sense they're capable of rehabilitation and difficulty out all of their incredible inclinations and triumphs.

SEARCH FOR STRATEGIES TO EMPOWER YOUR LOVED ONE.

Rather than doing matters for them that they're capable of doing for themselves, it's most suitable to growth their self belief and self-bear in mind thru supplying them with more options and control.

ANTICIPATE AND MANAGE TRIGGERS

A purpose is a few thing—a person, vicinity, item, or state of affairs—that reminds your cherished one of the trauma and triggers off a PTSD symptom, together with a flashback. Occasionally, triggers are obtrusive. For instance, a navy veteran can be precipitated through the use of seeing his warmates or thru the loud sounds that appear like firing. Some can also additionally make an effort to understand and recognize, which includes listening to a music that have end up playing even as the disturbing incident took place, for example, so now that song or maybe others within the same musical fashion are triggers. Similarly, triggers do no longer need to be external. Internal sentiments and sensations should in all likelihood doubtlessly initiate PTSD symptoms and signs.

Common External PTSD Triggers:

Sights, sounds, or odours related with the trauma.

Persons, locations, or things that evoke the trauma.

Important dates or durations, together with anniversaries or a positive time of day.

Nature (various types of climate, seasons, and so on). (fine sorts of weather, seasons, and so on.).

Discussions or media coverage concerning trauma or ugly facts occurrences.

Circumstances that appear limiting (stuck in website traffic, at the medical doctor's place of job, in a throng).

Relationship, own family, school, hobby, or cash needs or disputes.

Funerals, hospitals, or hospital treatment.

Common Internal PTSD Triggers:

Physical discomforts, which includes hunger, thirst, exhaustion, contamination, and sexual dissatisfaction.

Anybody experience that remembers the event, which incorporates pain, preceding wounds and scars, or a similar damage.

Intense emotions, specially feeling powerless, out of manipulate, or imprisoned.

Emotions towards circle of relatives participants include contradictory sentiments of affection, vulnerability, and hatred.

TALKING TO YOUR LOVED ONE ABOUT PTSD TRIGGERS

Ask the one which you love about topics they've finished within the beyond to react to a trigger that seemed to assist (similarly to people who didn't). Then give you a collaborative activity plan for a way you could react in destiny.

Discuss with your beloved the way you should react when they go through a nightmare, flashback, or panic assault. Having a technique in place will make the state of affairs a whole lot much less terrifying for every of you. You'll moreover be in a far better characteristic to help the only which you love loosen up.

HOW TO ASSIST SOMEONE SUFFERING A FLASHBACK OR PANIC ATTACK

During a flashback, human beings usually have a sensation of disassociation, as though they are divorced from their personal body. Everything you may do to "floor" them will help.

Inform the only which you love they may be experiencing a flashback and that although it seems right, the incident is not simply happening once more.

Help remind them of their surroundings (as an instance, encourage them to go searching the room and supply an cause of out loud what they check) (for instance, ask them to go searching the room and describe out loud what they see).

Urge them to take deep, steady breaths (hyperventilating can accentuate feelings of panic).

Avoid fast actions or some thing that can shock them.

Ask before you contact them. Touching or putting your fingers around the man or woman have to cause them to sense imprisoned, that might result in accelerated inflammation or perhaps violence.

TIP five: DEAL WITH VOLATILITY AND ANGER

PTSD may additionally moreover cause hassle controlling feelings and impulses. In your beloved, this will end up excessive infection, moodiness, or eruptions of fury.

Individuals suffering from PTSD stay in a perpetual kingdom of physical and highbrow pressure. Because they regularly have problems sound asleep, it method they will be constantly weary, on component, and bodily strung out—increasing the opportunity that they may overreact to daily pressures.

For many people with PTSD, rage can also be a cover for one of a type emotions which includes loss, helplessness, or guilt. Rage makes people feel strong, in vicinity of vulnerable and defenceless. Some attempt to hide their wrath till it emerges whilst you least count on it.

Look for indicators that the only that you love is furious, collectively with tightening jaw or fists, speaking loudly, or growing impatient. Take motion to defuse the scenario as speedy as you take a look at the earliest warning symptoms.

STRIVE TO STAY CALM.

During an emotional outburst, do your remarkable to hold cool. This will illustrate to the one you love which you are "stable," and avoid the problem from escalating.

GIVE THE INDIVIDUAL ROOM.

Avoid crowding or greedy the person. This should in all likelihood make a traumatized character enjoy threatened.

INQUIRE HOW YOU CAN ASSIST.

For instance: "What can I do that will help you right now?" You can also moreover recommend a day trip or exchange of environment.

PUT SAFETY FIRST.

If the person grows greater livid however your efforts to calm her or him down, leave the house or lock your self in a room. Contact the police in case you fear that the one you love may moreover moreover injure himself or others.

HELP YOUR LOVED ONE REGULATE THEIR RAGE.

Anger is a herbal, healthful emotion, however when persistent, explosive rage spirals out of control, it is able to have essential implications for a person's relationships, health, and nation of mind. Your loved one might also moreover deliver anger underneath control by way of using expertise the vital reasons and adopting better strategies to specific their frustrations.

TIP 6: SUPPORT TREATMENT

Despite the fee of your love and assist, it isn't normally enough. Many human beings who have been traumatized require expert PTSD counseling. Yet bringing it up is probably uncomfortable. Consider the manner you'd feel if a person recommended which you required remedy.

WAIT FOR THE PROPER MOMENT TO SHARE YOUR CONCERNS.

Don't carry it up on the equal time as you're bickering or in the thick of a crisis. Additionally, be cautious together with your terminology. Avoid some aspect that suggests that the only that you love is "crazy." Frame it in a notable, sensible mild: remedy is a hazard to benefit new talents that may be done to address a significant form of PTSD-associated troubles.

HIGHLIGHT THE POSITIVES.

For instance, remedy may additionally additionally moreover help kids become more unbiased and in charge. Maybe it may assist reduce the tension and avoidance this is preventing them from attractive inside the subjects they want to do.

CONCENTRATE ON PARTICULAR ISSUES.

If the only that you love closes down whilst you communicate approximately PTSD or remedy, pay interest as an alternative on how treatment may additionally help with particular problems like anger manage, tension, or interest and memory issues.

Chapter 4: Complementary & Alternative (Cam) Treatment For Ptsd

UNDERSTANDING WHAT COMPLEMENTARY AND ALTERNATIVE TREATMENT FOR PTSD ARE

Complementary and opportunity treatments for PTSD (Post-traumatic pressure sickness) are trying to find advice from non-conventional strategies that aim to reduce signs and decorate high-quality of lifestyles for the ones laid low with the situation.

While conventional recuperation approaches like medication and psychotherapy are commonly used to deal with PTSD, a few human beings discover that complementary and possibility remedies also can be beneficial. Here are some common examples:

MIND-BODY PRACTICES: These consist of strategies like yoga, meditation, and tai chi. These practices can help lessen strain, tension, and depression, which might be regularly associated with PTSD.

ACUPUNCTURE: This is a shape of conventional Chinese medicinal drug that includes placing needles into specific points on the body. Some studies have cautioned that acupuncture can help lessen PTSD signs and symptoms like anxiety and insomnia.

EYE MOVEMENT DESENSITIZATION AND REPROCESSING (EMDR): EMDR is a psychotherapy method that includes recalling worrying sports at the same time as focusing on a therapist's hand moves or outstanding sorts of bilateral stimulation. Some studies recommend that EMDR can help reduce PTSD signs.

HERBAL SUPPLEMENTS: Some herbs, like St. John's wort and valerian root, are idea to have calming outcomes at the body and may be beneficial in reducing signs and symptoms of PTSD.

ANIMAL-ASSISTED THERAPY: This entails running with animals, consisting of dogs or horses, to assist lessen pressure and anxiety.

Animal-assisted remedy may be mainly useful for people who have experienced trauma.

It is critical to notice that at the identical time as those treatments can be useful for a few human beings, they're not an opportunity choice to traditional treatments like medication and psychotherapy. It is vital to speak to a healthcare professional approximately which remedies can be fine for your specific desires.

ART AND MUSIC THERAPY AS A MEANS OF COPING WITH PTSD

Art and music remedy can be effective manner of coping with PTSD (publish-worrying stress sickness) because they interact exceptional additives of the brain than conventional speak treatment, bearing in mind more emotional expression and processing.

Art treatment consists of the usage of diverse art work materials in conjunction with paints, pastels, or clay, to create photographs or devices that specific feelings and research related to the trauma. The way of making artwork can help humans get right of entry to and specific feelings that may be hard to place into terms. Additionally, the act of creating a few aspect tangible can offer a experience of manipulate and mastery over the disturbing enjoy.

Music remedy consists of the use of song and sound to sell emotional, cognitive, and bodily recuperation. It can involve listening to track, creating a music, gambling devices, or composing tune. Music treatment can provide a strong and nonverbal manner to explicit feelings and may help individuals alter their feelings, lessen anxiety, and beautify everyday temper.

Both paintings and tune remedy can also assist people increase coping abilities and boom self-interest, that may result in superior vanity and more resilience. These treatments can be used by myself or in combination with different varieties of treatment, consisting of medication and talk treatment.

It is essential to phrase that at the same time as paintings and song treatment can be useful for humans with PTSD, they're now not an opportunity to proof-primarily based clearly remedies such as cognitive-behavioral treatment (CBT) and medicinal drug. These healing methods need for use as a part of a complete remedy plan underneath the guidance of a mental fitness expert.

HYPNOTHERAPY FOR THE TREATMENT OF PTSD SYMPTOMS

Hypnotherapy can be a beneficial adjunct to traditional remedies for PTSD, collectively with remedy and psychotherapy. Hypnotherapy can assist people with PTSD via allowing them to access and tool disturbing memories in a secure and managed environment, in addition to help them enlarge coping abilties and decorate their cutting-edge revel in of nicely-being.

During hypnotherapy intervals, the therapist will manual the patient right right into a country of deep rest, that can assist to lessen anxiety and promote a sense of calmness. Once the affected individual is on this state, the therapist can also additionally use a whole lot of techniques to help them get right of entry to and reprocess demanding reminiscences, which include visualization and guided imagery.

One particular method this is often applied in hypnotherapy for PTSD is called "hypnotic desensitization," which incorporates exposing the affected person to a slow, controlled exposure to traumatic memories at the same time as in a hypnotic kingdom. The therapist can assist the affected individual artwork thru those reminiscences in a regular and controlled surroundings, that may help to reduce the depth of the emotional response to the trauma.

Research has verified that hypnotherapy may be an effective remedy for PTSD signs and symptoms, together with intrusive mind, flashbacks, and avoidance behaviors. However, it's far critical to be conscious that hypnotherapy ought to constantly be used collectively with exclusive evidence-primarily based remedies, which embody medicinal drug and psychotherapy, as a part of a whole treatment plan for PTSD. It is also essential to paintings with a certified and educated hypnotherapist who has experience working with humans with PTSD.

MINDFULNESS-BASED THERAPIES FOR PTSD

Post-worrying pressure ailment (PTSD) is a intellectual fitness condition which can growth after a person has expert or witnessed a annoying event. The signs and symptoms of PTSD can embody flashbacks, nightmares, avoidance behaviors, hyperarousal, and terrible modifications in temper and wondering. While PTSD can be a debilitating situation, there are various powerful remedies to be had, together with mindfulness-based completely treatments.

Mindfulness-based definitely treatments are a set of recuperation methods that incorporate the workout of mindfulness meditation as a full-size detail. Mindfulness meditation consists of listening to the existing 2nd, non-judgmentally, and with interest and recognition. This exercise can help human beings with PTSD become greater aware of their mind and feelings and take a look at to relate to them in a greater accepting and lots much less reactive way.

Several mindfulness-based totally treatments have been advanced for the remedy of PTSD, which includes mindfulness-based absolutely strain reduction (MBSR), mindfulness-based totally completely cognitive remedy (MBCT), and recognition and determination remedy (ACT). These healing strategies percentage a focus on developing mindfulness competencies to assist people with PTSD higher control their symptoms and signs and symptoms.

Mindfulness-Based Stress Reduction (MBSR) is a set up eight-week utility that includes mindfulness meditation, mild yoga, and agency speak. In MBSR, people learn how to have a look at their thoughts and emotions with out judgment, domesticate self-compassion, and make bigger a greater experience of reputation of the existing 2nd. Studies have proven that MBSR can be effective in lowering signs and symptoms of PTSD and enhancing satisfactory of existence in people with PTSD.

Mindfulness-Based Cognitive Therapy (MBCT) is a dependent 8-week software application that combines mindfulness meditation with cognitive behavioral therapy techniques. MBCT objectives to help individuals with PTSD choose out and task horrible idea styles that make contributions to their symptoms and signs. By cultivating mindfulness abilties, humans with PTSD can learn how to observe their mind and emotions without turning into beaten through them. Studies have shown that MBCT can be effective in decreasing signs and symptoms and signs and symptoms and signs and signs and symptoms of PTSD and enhancing elegant mental functioning.

Acceptance and Commitment Therapy (ACT) is a mindfulness-primarily based treatment that focuses on growing intellectual flexibility. ACT teaches human beings with PTSD to truely take delivery of their thoughts and feelings, even supposing they will be unpleasant, and to do so consistent with their values and goals. By cultivating mindfulness abilties, people with PTSD can learn how to have a have a have a look at their mind and emotions without turning into caught up in them. Studies have validated that ACT can be effective in decreasing signs and symptoms and signs and symptoms and signs and symptoms of PTSD and enhancing commonplace functioning.

In conclusion, mindfulness-based totally definitely remedy options are powerful remedies for PTSD that could assist people broaden skills to control their signs and symptoms and symptoms and signs and symptoms and signs. By cultivating mindfulness competencies, individuals with PTSD can learn how to have a examine their thoughts and emotions without becoming crushed through using them, predominant to a complicated splendid of existence. If you or a person you apprehend is suffering with PTSD, it's miles critical to searching out expert assist and endure in thoughts mindfulness-primarily based totally treatment plans as a treatment desire.

Chapter 5: Ptsd & Diet

THE RELATIONSHIP BETWEEN NUTRITION AND PTSD SYMPTOMS

Post-Traumatic Stress Disorder (PTSD) is a intellectual fitness situation that could boom after experiencing or witnessing a stressful occasion. The symptoms and signs and symptoms of PTSD may be debilitating and encompass flashbacks, nightmares, tension, depression, and hyperarousal. The dating amongst vitamins and PTSD symptoms has been studied in state-of-the-art years, and research suggests that there may be a connection between the two.

Firstly, it's crucial to apprehend the effect of stress on the frame. When the frame reports pressure, it activates the hypothalamic-pituitary-adrenal (HPA) axis and sympathetic involved tool (SNS). This ends inside the launch of cortisol and adrenaline, which can impact the body's metabolism and nutrient absorption. Chronic stress can reason dysregulation of the HPA axis and SNS, most important to nutrient deficiencies, inflammation, and oxidative stress.

Research has proven that humans with PTSD have better prices of nutrient deficiencies in assessment to the overall population. Specifically, PTSD has been connected to lower stages of food regimen D, eating regimen B6, nutrition B12, folate, and omega-3 fatty acids. These nutrients are essential for regulating mood, lowering infection, and enhancing cognitive feature. Low tiers of those nutrients also can exacerbate PTSD signs and signs and boom the threat of developing comorbidities which includes depression and anxiety.

Additionally, research has demonstrated that PTSD can effect urge for food and food picks. Individuals with PTSD can also moreover have a reduced urge for meals, predominant to weight loss and nutrient deficiencies. On the alternative hand, a few people may also moreover flip to comfort ingredients immoderate in sugar and fats, leading to weight benefit and ability nutrient imbalances. These nutritional changes can similarly effect temper and cognitive feature, exacerbating PTSD signs.

There is likewise evidence to signify that nutritional interventions may additionally additionally moreover decorate PTSD symptoms and signs and symptoms and signs. For instance, studies have established that omega-three supplementation can reduce signs and symptoms and signs of hysteria and depression in human beings with PTSD. Additionally, a Mediterranean-fashion diet rich in fruits, vegetables, whole grains, lean protein, and healthful fat has been shown to enhance mood and cognitive function in human beings with despair and tension, which can also be applicable to PTSD.

In give up, there may be a complex courting among nutrients and PTSD symptoms. Nutrient deficiencies and dietary adjustments also can exacerbate PTSD symptoms and signs and symptoms, at the identical time as nutritional interventions can also additionally enhance symptoms and symptoms and signs and symptoms. Therefore, it's miles crucial to bear in mind the effect of nutrients on intellectual health and to address any nutrient deficiencies or dietary imbalances inside the remedy of PTSD.

HOW DIET CAN AFFECT PTSD TRIGGERS AND FLASHBACKS

While there are numerous treatments to be had for PTSD, together with remedy and medicine, the function of weight loss program in managing PTSD signs and signs and signs is becoming increasingly more recognized. Studies have tested that positive meals and vitamins can have an effect on the mind and frightened device and may play a characteristic in PTSD triggers and flashbacks.

Here are a few processes wherein diet regime can affect PTSD triggers and flashbacks:

BLOOD SUGAR LEVELS:

Research has established that low blood sugar stages can cause signs of tension and panic, that could exacerbate PTSD signs and symptoms. Eating meals at regular intervals and eating meals that release glucose slowly, consisting of complex carbohydrates and fiber, can help stabilize blood sugar levels and reduce the threat of triggers.

CAFFEINE:

Caffeine, determined in espresso, tea, and power liquids, is a stimulant that would boom anxiety and reason flashbacks in people with PTSD. Reducing or averting caffeine intake can help manipulate PTSD signs and symptoms and signs.

ALCOHOL:

Alcohol can intrude with sleep, boom anxiety and despair, and impair cognitive functioning. Alcohol use also can make it more hard to cope with PTSD symptoms and boom the danger of flashbacks. Reducing or keeping off alcohol intake is usually encouraged for people with PTSD.

OMEGA-3 FATTY ACIDS:

Omega-three fatty acids, placed in fatty fish, nuts, and seeds, are crucial for mind feature and may help reduce contamination within the thoughts. Some research recommend that omega-3 nutritional nutritional supplements may additionally assist lessen PTSD signs and symptoms and symptoms, in particular hyperarousal and tension.

MAGNESIUM:

Magnesium is a mineral that performs a important role inside the stressful device, assisting to alter pressure hormones and neurotransmitters. Some research recommend that magnesium supplementation can also additionally help reduce anxiety and hyperarousal signs and symptoms in humans with PTSD.

B VITAMINS:

B nutrients, which include thiamine, riboflavin, and niacin, are essential for thoughts feature and can help modify mood and decrease tension. Some studies advocate that B weight loss program supplementation may additionally assist reduce PTSD signs and symptoms and signs and symptoms, including despair and anxiety.

In precis, weight-reduction plan can play a excellent function in handling PTSD signs and symptoms, which include triggers and flashbacks. Eating a balanced healthy eating plan that includes complicated carbohydrates, fiber, omega-3 fatty acids, and magnesium, and decreasing or fending off caffeine and alcohol consumption can assist stabilize blood sugar levels, lessen infection, and alter strain hormones and neurotransmitters, which may additionally assist alleviate PTSD symptoms and signs and symptoms. It is crucial to are in search of for advice from a healthcare expert in advance than making any nutritional modifications or taking nutritional supplements to govern PTSD signs and symptoms.

STRATEGIES FOR MAINTAINING A HEALTHY DIET WHILE COPING WITH PTSD

Coping with PTSD may be hard, and maintaining a healthy food plan is an critical thing of self-care that could assist manage signs and signs and symptoms and promote standard nicely being. Here are a few techniques for retaining a healthful food regimen even as managing PTSD:

PRACTICE MINDFUL EATING: Mindful consuming includes being gift and genuinely engaged with the revel in of eating. It manner being attentive to the flavor, smell, texture, and coloration of the food, similarly to the feelings and sensations that rise up even as ingesting. This can help people with PTSD live grounded in the gift second and keep away from using food as a coping mechanism.

PLAN MEALS IN ADVANCE: Planning food earlier can assist people with PTSD keep away from the strain of having to make picks about what to eat while they may be already feeling crushed. This can also help make sure that they have pretty a few nutritious food to be had that might help their bodily and emotional fitness.

CHOOSE NUTRIENT-DENSE FOODS: Nutrient-dense meals are individuals who offer a excessive quantity of nutrients for their calorie content material. These meals can assist individuals with PTSD revel in complete and satisfied whilst additionally supporting their traditional health. Examples of nutrient-dense food consist of fruits, veggies, lean protein resources, and whole grains.

AVOID RESTRICTIVE DIETS: Restrictive diets may be annoying and might exacerbate signs and symptoms and signs of PTSD. Instead, individuals with PTSD have to recognition on eating a balanced and sundry eating regimen that consists of an entire lot of elements from all food corporations.

INCORPORATE SELF-CARE PRACTICES: Self-care practices, together with meditation, deep respiratory, and yoga, can help humans with PTSD manage strain and reduce emotional ingesting. By looking after their emotional nicely-being, people with PTSD can higher manipulate their signs and symptoms and symptoms and make healthier meals picks.

SEEK SUPPORT: Seeking guide from a mental health expert or a registered dietitian can be beneficial for people with PTSD who are suffering to maintain a wholesome diet. These specialists can provide steerage and aid to help human beings make more healthy meals alternatives and develop coping techniques for coping with pressure and emotional ingesting.

In conclusion, keeping a wholesome weight loss plan is an important aspect of self-deal with human beings with PTSD. By training conscious consuming, making plans food earlier, deciding on nutrient-dense food, retaining off restrictive diets, incorporating self-care practices, and looking for assist, people with PTSD can beneficial resource their everyday health and manipulate their symptoms.

FOODS TO EAT AND AVOID WHEN YOU HAVE PTSD

Post-demanding strain disorder (PTSD) is a highbrow fitness scenario which could amplify after experiencing or witnessing a stressful event. While food by myself cannot treatment PTSD, it may play a role in helping to control the situation.

Here are some materials to devour and avoid when you have PTSD:

Chapter 6: What Is Emotional Trauma

Emotional trauma refers to intense intellectual distress that consequences from a disturbing occasion or series of events, which includes abuse, forget about, harassment or publicity to violence.

Emotional trauma can also have a profound and lasting impact on a person's highbrow fitness and well-being, causing emotions of fear, anxiety, guilt, and shame, similarly to bodily signs and symptoms together with insomnia, complications, and digestive troubles.

Emotional or intellectual trauma is a reaction to a annoying occasion that influences your feelings.

Emotional trauma may also have an impact on people of all ages and backgrounds and is not restricted to the ones who've expert physical violent sports. It moreover may be attributable to an lousy lot an awful lot less overt kinds of trauma, on the facet of emotional abuse or forget.

It is important for humans who've expert emotional trauma to are searching for assist and assist, including remedy or counseling, to system and heal from their reminiscences. With the right care, humans can research coping mechanisms to control their symptoms and lead a satisfying existence.

Emotional trauma is a form of intellectual harm that effects from rather distressing occasions on the facet of bodily, sexual, or emotional abuse, witnessing violence, or losing a cherished one. It may also moreover have lasting consequences on a person's highbrow and emotional well-being, affecting their relationships, behavior, and shallowness.

Traumatic research can weigh down an individual's capability to cope, leaving them feeling helpless, powerless, and on my own. These emotions can motive excessive feelings consisting of fear, anger, guilt, and disgrace that persist lengthy after the worrying occasion has ended.

If left untreated, emotional trauma can motive the development of highbrow health conditions collectively with put up-worrying stress sickness (PTSD), despair, tension, and substance abuse. However, with right resource and treatment, humans can get over emotional trauma and discover ways to manage its outcomes

Emotional trauma refers to a deep and lasting intellectual wound because of a big event or series of activities that weigh down an man or woman's capacity to govern. It can surrender cease end result from a unmarried demanding experience, collectively with a natural catastrophe, bodily attack, or sexual abuse, or from ongoing exposure to disturbing situations, which incorporates dwelling in an abusive household or serving in combat.

We usually apprehend trauma due to a few problem violent, like a vehicle coincidence or the occasions professional with the aid of squaddies at some point of combat.

But trauma can be extra nuanced, and while natural screw ups like floods, hurricanes and earthquakes can honestly purpose trauma (as can mass shootings and terrorist assaults), emotional trauma additionally can be resulting from a long manner extra diffused activities or research.

Emotional traumas generally healthy a specific framework: as an instance, trauma on your emotions or emotions, because of abuse or overlook approximately. Emotional trauma can go away you feeling hazardous and worrying, and while left unaddressed, can become continual.

It's crucial to observe that everyone reacts in every other manner to trauma, and what might be worrying for one person may not be for every different.

Furthermore, the results of trauma can very last for years, and might moreover be passed down from generation to era

Emotional trauma can motive immoderate and prolonged-lasting emotions of fear, anxiety, disgrace, guilt, anger, and powerlessness. It can also have physical outcomes, consisting of complications, insomnia, and adjustments in appetite.

 The mental and bodily signs and symptoms of emotional trauma can intrude with an individual's each day lifestyles and relationships, and may cause the development of mental health troubles which include depression, put up-traumatic strain disorder (PTSD), and anxiety troubles.

(1.2); The generation inside the again of a damaged heart

When we revel in emotional heartache or a "damaged coronary coronary heart," it may feel like a bodily ache. However, this revel in is simply the quit end result of complex methods in the mind and frame.

Going through emotional trauma or grief— every of which can be being professional through tens of thousands and thousands of human beings these days—can leave a long lasting imprint on the mind and may cause a laundry list of signs and symptoms and signs and symptoms. You may also enjoy sad, unable to pay attention, edgy, demanding, or irritable, and might have problem napping.

Often, grief is mislabeled as despair, ADD/ADHD, panic sickness, or other psychiatric situations.

And put up-demanding stress disease (PTSD), which influences many people who enjoy trauma, is regularly misdiagnosed as a disturbing mind harm (TBI) due to the fact they've overlapping symptoms.

When we revel in intense emotions, inclusive of grief or rejection, our thoughts releases stress hormones, along side cortisol and adrenaline.

These hormones reason the combat-or-flight reaction, which can reason physical signs and symptoms collectively with increased coronary heart fee, chest ache, and shortness of breath. These signs and symptoms and signs can mimic the revel in of a coronary coronary heart attack, therefore the sensation of a "broken coronary heart."

Heartbreak is an unluckily common part of the human enjoy, and it in reality, in reality sucks. We've all been there, and it's steady to say all of us need to keep away from experiencing heartbreak ever all over again.

We experience coronary heart damaged while we lose someone or something we cherished or wanted very lots, like a romantic courting or a friendship, a family member, a pet, or a pastime or possibility that became very critical to us.

This is difficult because of the fact in case you're misdiagnosed, psychotropic drug treatments can get within the way of healing and in some times, can lengthen grief and emotional trauma. If you enjoy lingering signs and symptoms and symptoms related to trauma or a loss, bear in mind doing grief work earlier than taking remedy.

Heartbreak can purpose a big quantity of strain, mainly if the loss is a shocking one. This stress will have an impact on how we experience emotionally and bodily, and might take weeks, months or perhaps years to recover from.

While there's nonetheless loads to find out approximately how and why we revel in love and heartbreak and the effect those have on our our our bodies, scientific take a look at has furnished us with some clues about why heartbreak makes you experience so garbage, and a few techniques to apply in case you're feeling genuinely down.

Additionally, emotional strain can also effect the function of the autonomic nervous device, which regulates the body's unconscious features, which encompass respiration and heartbeat.

This can bring about modifications to the coronary coronary coronary heart rate and blood strain, in addition contributing to bodily symptoms and signs.In some cases, the stress and emotional trauma of a broken heart also can weaken the immune system, making human beings greater susceptible to infection.

It's essential to maintain in thoughts that on the same time as the experience of a broken coronary coronary heart can experience very actual and physical, it's far a brief situation and commonly resolves on its non-public over the years with proper self-care and manual.

(1.Three); A medically broken coronary heart

Ever puzzled if emotional heartbreak can really, physical harm your heart?

A medically broken coronary coronary heart refers to a condition referred to as "Takotsubo cardiomyopathy" or "Broken Heart Syndrome."

Takotsubo Cardiomyopathy is the scientific call for a syndrome that can be due to heartbreak, or more as it need to be, the strain of a heartbreaking scenario.

This is a situation that mimics a coronary heart assault, however rather is due to emotional or bodily pressure. The scenario can reason a unexpected and brief weakening of the coronary heart muscle, essential to coronary heart failure.

The symptoms of broken coronary coronary heart syndrome can embody chest ache, shortness of breath, and an atypical heartbeat. The unique cause of the circumstance isn't always yet completely understood, however it's far believed to be related to a surge of pressure hormones, which incorporates adrenaline, which could cause modifications within the coronary heart muscle.

Broken coronary heart syndrome is typically taken into consideration to be a benign and reversible situation, and most human beings make a whole recovery internal a few weeks. However, in uncommon instances, it can result in greater immoderate complications, which includes coronary heart failure or cardiogenic marvel.

If you suspect you may be experiencing damaged coronary heart syndrome, it's far essential to are looking for clinical attention right away, because of the fact the signs and symptoms may be similar to the ones of a coronary coronary coronary heart assault.

Treatment normally involves medicines to manual the coronary heart and manipulate symptoms and signs, in addition to dealing with the underlying strain or emotional reason that may have brought on the situation.

Acute emotional pressure, first rate or terrible, can cause the left ventricle of the coronary heart to be 'bowled over' or paralysed, inflicting coronary heart assault-like signs such as robust chest, arm or shoulder pains, shortness of breath, dizziness, loss of popularity, nausea and vomiting.

The top information: the state of affairs doesn't commonly reason eternal harm like a coronary heart attack does, and often resolves itself. The awful statistics: it could be annoying and painful, with humans regularly thinking they're having an actual coronary heart assault.

A medically broken coronary coronary coronary heart, additionally referred to as "broken coronary coronary heart syndrome" or stress-induced cardiomyopathy, is a situation wherein someone reports sudden, intense chest pain and shortness of breath due to a surge of stress hormones.

The state of affairs can mimic the signs of a coronary coronary heart assault, however it is not because of blockages in the coronary arteries. Instead, it is idea to be because of the results of stress hormones at the coronary heart muscle.

84

Broken coronary coronary heart syndrome is usually seen in people who have experienced a worrying occasion, which encompass the loss of life of a cherished one, a divorce, or a demanding occasion.

Women are much more likely to revel in broken coronary coronary heart syndrome, and the scenario is generally brief and resolves on its very own inside some days to weeks.

Treatment for broken coronary heart syndrome commonly consists of supportive care, which incorporates bed rest, medicinal drugs to alleviate symptoms and signs, and measures to control pressure. In severe times, someone may additionally need to be hospitalized and handled with medicinal drugs to assist their coronary coronary heart characteristic.

If you believe you studied you'll be experiencing signs and signs and symptoms of broken coronary coronary heart syndrome, it's far vital to are on the lookout for for scientific hobby right away. Your clinical health practitioner can perform checks to determine the reason of your symptoms and signs and symptoms and advocate the first-class path of treatment for you.

Need to understand

The reality of the manner painful a broken coronary coronary coronary heart can be first hit me many years in the past. I understand the term we use is heartbroken but, at the same time as my relationship ended, I simply felt broken, punched in the intestine.

I were at that risky juncture of being really loved-up and definitely unprepared.

And nearly worse than the surprise became how embarrassed I felt. My internal voice saved telling me to place this in perspective and thru hook or by way of manner of criminal rally spherical.

But new findings on heartbreak show it's far a physiological and highbrow kingdom. Rather than a few element to belittle, heartbreak is a profound form of grief. I wasn't being stupid; I end up experiencing the confirmed effect of romantic loss.

One of the first reassuring quantities of research I even have a take a look at, at the same time as looking for to grapple with the complex aftermath of my private depressing breakup, have become a high look at of studies on heartbreak thru the psychologist Tiffany Field on the University of Miami.

She had pulled collectively findings from a number of distinct researchers showing that the symptoms and signs and symptoms of heartbreak resembled those of bereavement: sleep disturbance, compromised immune function, digestive issues, frame aches, depression, tension, all the way to some component known as 'broken-coronary coronary heart syndrome' in which the surprise from loss can result in a coronary coronary heart assault-style episode.

At least I knew I wasn't regressing to my melodramatic teenage self; someone had vanished and the loss hit me tough. If, like me, you have got been stressed by using the use of the pressure of the blow, it'd assist to do not forget heartbreak in this manner.

Not handiest did I feel sad and out of area and pressured and weepy, I additionally felt physically ill.

I keep in mind sitting in a brightly lit diner with my extremely good friend, some days after my breakup, watching my plate of meals now not able to consume. The scent of meals, even the idea of it, changed into genuinely off-placing.

I am now not someone who ever misses a meal, however proper right here I modified into feeling unwell to my belly like I had gastric flu. I notion we without a doubt talked about being lovesick: I didn't anticipate I grow to be in fact going to hurry to the rest room to throw up.

One of the primary reasons we feel so ill within the aftermath of a breakup is the strain of rejection, betrayal and loss, essential to the release of the stress hormone cortisol.

Extra cortisol in moments of chance is specifically useful. It turns on our our our our bodies and gets us equipped to defend ourselves or flee the scene.

The fight-or-flight reaction (also known as the extreme pressure reaction) is in which a shape of domino effect occurs internal us, our mind perceives a danger, our body hears the cry for help and releases strain hormones in response to this danger.

But if we don't want to actually fight or run for our lives, then we can be left with a few unpleasant aspect-outcomes. Our muscular tissues (if not used to beat back that grizzly go through) can grow to be worrying and taut, generating aches and pains.

If you feel including you've been hit via the use of a truck proper now, then this might be why. Cortisol and different hormones moreover teach our bodies to divert blood an extended way from our digestive gadget as a way to make certain that our muscle businesses have accurate enough blood supply to fuel our fight-or-flight united states of america of the united states.

This diversion can relatively upset our digestive gadget, triggering belly aches, diarrhea or lack of urge for food.

The broken-hearted revel in like they may be falling aside, however they may be certainly having a regular bodily reaction to the flood of cortisol induced with the aid of the stress.

The broken-hearted additionally crave the neurotransmitter and hormone dopamine, generated with the resource of the body even as we're 'in love'. Dopamine is produced within the brain's reward centre, the region that generates pleasure and motivation.

Chapter 7: How To Recover From Emotional Trauma;

There's a few discouraging information in terms of healing: Recovering from emotional traumas is a notable deal more of a technique than a short-healing answer. In all risk, your emotional trauma will make an effort to cope with in a significant way.

So how does one get over emotional trauma?

Well, it could be a rely of time. Experts have visible that, for maximum people, a demanding event's results will usually reduce over time. It's similar to how the ache of a damage-up can fade with time.

That takes region with trauma responses as properly for plenty humans.It's essential to make clear that, regardless of what many human beings have wrongfully idea in the past, you can not numb the ache, nor are you capable of speed up time via abusing pills or alcohol.

In fact, these are matters you need to actively keep away from while handling the aftermath of a demanding occasion.

What should you do alternatively?

Take care of yourself, and particularly your mind and body. The NIMH says that you can do this thru preserving sports. You may want to hold normal physical activities for food, exercising and sleep — all of that may help mitigate the possibly harmful outcomes of trauma.

Keeping yourself on a schedule will lessen down on that unsure time while negative mind can fill area.You additionally shouldn't spend too much time by myself.

The NIMH says that spending time with buddies, loved ones, and exclusive relied on people of your social circles who are supportive is an effective way to paintings through the coping period, but long it could take for you.

Generally speakme, this complete gadget may be considered a shape of self-care — and a manner of coping with the horrible thoughts on the equal time as preserving your thoughts and frame healthful.

Taking care of your body has additionally been validated to help with emotional restoration.

Lastly, in case you don't experience that topics are improving, or if you're feeling remoted, or perhaps if subjects do appear to be improving and you actually want to invite a few questions, we endorse talking to a highbrow fitness professional approximately medicinal drug or treatment.

Therapy is arguably as beneficial and critical to your thoughts as an annual physical to your frame, or an oil trade to your automobile.

Licensed therapists and different mental fitness organizations are able to offering you with advice or referrals for what you're suffering with.

What to do,

Accept your feeling

One soothing exercising you can try in the ones first few complicated weeks is a touch splendor of the manner you revel in. This is a way taken from popularity and dedication treatment (ACT) and is based at the idea that, if we deliver ourselves permission to sense but we enjoy, without self-judgment, it can help us to procedure some thing we're struggling with.

The idea is to awareness your thoughts on a clean assertion that articulates your feelings. This can be 'It's k to enjoy unhappy,' or 'You are not on my own in being heartbroken,' or 'It's suitable sufficient to like someone you're not with.'In the ones moments, we acquire our emotions as legitimate, no longer silly or negative.

A contemporary study from the Neurocognition of Emotion and Motivation Lab on the University of Missouri-St Louis that used this approach on heartbroken human beings decided that focused on the ones styles of sentences a few seconds at a time reduced inspired interest for the ex-associate, which means that that the people have been less captivated thru their heartbreaker and in all likelihood a bit more free to transport on.

It wasn't that the ones people were no longer unhappy or heartbroken, however they had been loads a good deal much less obsessed with the useful useful resource of the ex.

This can be surprisingly beneficial if you are fixated on that character who has clearly rejected you.This method allows you to recognition at the triumphing without trying to overcome whatever. It can help to definitely get maintain of your current-day nation.

This can be achieved as a kind of meditative exercising, starting your days with a couple of minutes in that you allow yourself to be kind to your self and sincere approximately the manner you feel.

Find a quiet spot, offer your self this non violent 2nd and recognition on a smooth, real feeling, with out critiquing it, really allowing it to sink in, and rest there for a second.

Give your self permission to grieve

It can be tempting to try to 'maintain it collectively' at the same time as you're in surprise or struggling with terrible information. If you are capable of view this heartbreak as a shape of grief, then letting your self cry and mourn this loss may be an vital way to launch a number of the disappointment you sense.

How regularly have you ever ever heard the saying that 'grief is available in waves'? These waves are in all likelihood to glide outside and inside and, even though I recognize which you may not want to burst into tears at the same time as chairing a assembly or visiting domestic on a hectic commuter bus, you're likely to enjoy a lot worse if you try to hold this disappointment inner.

When you experience the ones waves of grief hit you, the exceptional thing you may do is to allow yourself cry or allow your self be open about how horrible you're feeling. You don't need to try to preserve this in with the resource of bottling up unhappiness or answering every 'How are you doing?' with a high-pitched 'I am absolutely high-quality!'

This is a time to attain out for help, be honest about how terrible you experience, and offer your self permission to address this drastically.

Maybe your inner voice is kinder than mine modified into, however I recognize I ought to regularly battle a very British stiff-better-lip mentality in that length. Cry in case you want to cry, and be honest approximately the way you enjoy. Reach out to buddies while you need them.

Allow yourself to grieve. Having your coronary heart damaged is painful. You can not get across the reality that it is going to damage.

You need to deliver your self time to sense the feelings related to heartache.

Your thoughts is telling you that you had been injured, so do not try to suppress those feelings.

[1]You will will be predisposed to cycle thru many emotions; anger, pain, grief, anxiety, fear, reputation.

[2] It can enjoy a bit like you're drowning at instances, but you could discover as you undergo each cycle, that you cope with them greater resultseasily and similarly rapid.

Avoid wallowing in despair. Let yourself cry. Crying is a wonderful issue. There is, but, a super line amongst giving yourself time to deal with your emotions and being absolutely overwhelmed via them.

If you discover you haven't left your house in weeks, have now not showered, and aren't interested by a few factor, you need to remember seeking out expert assist.

Counseling or participating in a few agency remedy can be the solution.

Get a few workout

There is a poster in my health club that asserts: 'When your frame is busy, your thoughts isn't.' Not groundbreaking, I realize, however it so surely summarises my enjoy of exercising. I can experience my mind smooth and the pressure ease as I exercise.

I could say it emerge as magical if I didn't realise there has been a huge amount of research on this area.

A important assessment of those research looked at facts from almost 20,000 human beings, and decided robust institutions among bodily hobby and decreased mental misery, with even moderate workout which include cleaning or gardening making a difference.

Even in case you apprehend all this deep down, it is able to be difficult to encourage yourself to get energetic at the same time as you're at your most heartbroken.

It is tempting to curve up and hibernate inside the starting, and clearly you may probably find that your motivation is low. This is not a time to overcome yourself up or to set unrealistic dreams.

Even genuinely setting clean, mild goals – maybe seeking out to get out for a 10-minute walk a day – can assist. Taking some little one steps in the path of developing your exercise will help. When you workout and growth your coronary heart charge, your cortisol degrees pass down, and, despite the fact that that is certainly with the useful aid of a small quantity at a time, it could assist ease the unsightly outcomes of strain you're experiencing.

Spend time in nature

The herbal global can be a type of remedy. The idea of 'woodland bathing' might likely sound like a modern-day style however in masses of cultures immersing in nature to lessen stress or disappointment isn't always a few factor new.

In Japan, it's miles been used for many years and, during the last 40 years, studies there has demonstrated that on foot in a wooded region cannot most effective assist whilst you are feeling low but additionally lower pressure stages, beautify attention or even growth the immune device. If you do no longer live subsequent to a lovable Japanese wooded location, then do now not fear.

Recent studies that tracked corporations of people walking in open, inexperienced spaces recorded that the ones strolling out in nature, as opposed to those in an urban surroundings, had a more boom in endorphins and further lower in cortisol levels.

Just taking walks in inexperienced regions can help us, and if we need to assist our low mood then having a lift from endorphins – a chemical produced through the frame that relieves stress and ache and might create a feel of euphoria – is well worth the diversion some distance from busy streets to natural environments.

Distract yourself

Distract yourself. After you've got gotten over the preliminary grieving way and treated your emotions, you need to spend a while distracting your self. Maybe you've got were given some interests you've got been ignoring. Perhaps you experience like doing some baking or running on crossword puzzles.

When your recollections of the your ex start to bubble up, distract yourself with every different idea or interest.

Call your buddy. Reach out to the buddy who stated to name on every occasion you needed to. Read a ebook you have got been which means that to get to for a while. Put on a humorous film (an delivered bonus, because of the truth laughter can help with the healing).

The lots much less you don't forget your ex and your heartache, the less difficult the recuperation approach may be. It takes artwork! It takes a aware and planned attempt into in reality redirecting your wondering and warding off considering your heartache.

Do now not take too many "painkillers". This will simplest mask the pain. Sometimes you truely surely need to take a harm from the physical pain. Be cautious, but, which you do no longer abuse those numbing exercises. In the start, you in reality do need to deal with your emotions.

"Painkillers" may be things like alcohol or pills, however it may moreover be such things as searching obsessive portions of t.V. Or in no way getting off the net, or binging on consolation meals.

One way of easing your thoughts after a breakup is thru the technique of distraction. The aforementioned have a take a look at from the University of Missouri-St Louis took heartbroken ladies and men and tested the use of distraction to ease misery.

Participants have been asked to actively distract their minds from mind in their heartbreak, through manner of specializing in topics unrelated to their breakup, such as their desired track or movies, or wherein they may need to tour subsequent.

The consequences showed that, after the usage of this approach, their health ratings were better and the exercising had a extremely good impact on their emotions and moods.

The distraction techniques used on this test have been thru and big about moving the thoughts to special, happier subjects so as no longer to stay on lousy mind, however distraction can be about throwing your self into an hobby too, or looking a movie. This is not to mention you shouldn't reflect onconsideration on your past dating in any respect.

Distraction strategies are not approximately suppressing memories or burying your feelings however alternatively redirecting your thoughts while some component is repeating on a loop for your thoughts.

Of path, you may although think about that man or woman and the relationship, but if those mind are overwhelming, as they often may be initially, then it may be soothing to provide your mind a rest.

It is commonplace to enjoy some form of despair following a breakup, with a few research displaying that as many as 40 consistent with cent of heartbroken human beings do so.

However, if this despair starts offevolved offevolved offevolved to turn out to be overwhelming, then a low mood which could have a look at loss have to tip into a few thing greater intense.

You need to try to alleviate this as plenty as possible via the usage of stopping your mind from dwelling an excessive amount of on the breakup.

Recovering from emotional trauma may be an prolonged and tough device, however it's far possible to heal and regain a revel in of manipulate over your existence. Here are a few steps that could help:

* Acknowledge Your Feelings

* Remove Reminders of Your Ex

* Find Closure

* Make a List of Your Ex's Faults

* Take Care of Yourself

We've all been there at one thing in our lives—those lousy days following the death of a dating at the same time as all you want to do is climb in mattress and pull the overs over your head.

 After all, breakups are never clean irrespective of whether or not you obtain dumped or you did the dumping.

Emotional trauma is a complicated state of affairs count, and one that's frequently misunderstood. Emotional traumas can and function befell to a lot of us, however in contrast to bodily traumas, the scars and accidents they go away inside the again of are not seen to anyone else.

"Breakups are tough. They can signify a trade in roles, ordinary, or even cause one to impeach their values of who they will be," explains Evita Limon-Rocha, MD, a infant, adolescent, and adult psychiatrist at Kaiser Permanente in Riverside, California.

"Acknowledging your feelings and normalizing the fashion of emotions skilled in this manner is high in allowing yourself to heal."

This leaves the healing system largely hidden, and the harm in huge part internalized, to the component that some people never apprehend they've skilled emotional trauma in the first region.

If you are like many humans, but, you likely do no longer address breakups in the healthiest of methods. Maybe you resort to drowning your sorrows with meals or beverages. Or, likely you can't prevent blaming yourself for the whole thing that went wrong. Whatever you are modern-day coping mechanisms, you're possibly questioning if there may be a better way to get thru this heartache.

Whether you're studying approximately this challenge count for yourself or a person else, the good facts is that you've taken one of the toughest steps in the restoration way with the resource of the use of being inclined to discover about your trauma. Even higher data: The subsequent steps are tons much less hard.

To help you placed the beyond in the back of you and waft on, we have were given compiled a listing of things you could do proper now to experience higher and help mend your broken coronary coronary coronary heart. So, do not waste some one-of-a-kind second wallowing within the past, and take steps to enjoy better right now.

The toughest element approximately managing emotional trauma is accepting that it occurred, and that help is desired.

Read immediately to observe greater about emotional trauma and a manner to get over it.

Acknowledge Your Feeling

While it's far quality natural to want to revel in better, you do not want to stuff your emotions or deny they even exist. Part of the recovery machine is acknowledging the manner you sense and allowing your self to grieve.

"It's important to famend your emotions of misery and grief after a breakup due to the fact it is a huge loss," explains Erin Pash LMFT, CEO of Ellie Mental Health. "We don't communicate enough about losses that aren't loss of life.

Ambiguous loss, like a breakup, is a loss that might often leave us looking for solutions if we don't take the time to paintings thru the complicated feelings of completing a courting."

This machine is critical if you are coming out of an extended-time period dating. Even if the connection modified into fraught with problems, you will probably even though experience like a part of you is lacking.

• Allow yourself the time and the gap to cry: Believe it or no longer, crying offers a launch on the manner to absolutely enhance your mood and assist you sense better ultimately.1 "It's furthermore unique sufficient to simply sit on your feelings and allow yourself sense terrible. Letting yourself have feelings is healthy notwithstanding the reality that awesome humans won't see it that manner. Crying, wallowing, and acknowledging pain is every now and then the remarkable medicine," Pash notes.

● Avoid getting caught: Healing after a breakup takes time, but it's miles important not to get mired down in this diploma of the healing approach. You want to allow yourself some time to method what happened. Remember that this approach appears one in each of a kind for every character. "There isn't any linear path within the face of grief, which encompass within the loss of a dating and this journey to restoration can be incredibly variable," Dr. Limon-Rocha explains.

● Talk to a expert: This isn't always to say that a pang of disappointment will not marvel you right here and there, but crying for days and days may be counterproductive to the recovery method. If you discover that you cannot stop crying or that you are crying for no obvious reason, you want to talk to your scientific physician or a counselor.

Not taking the time to broadly recognized your emotions and heal can create similarly issues. Sometimes, a demanding breakup can reason depression in some human beings or reignite a intellectual health hassle.

If you don't take the time to heal, depending on how massive the wound is, it can bleed into your future relationships in dangerous ways

Remove Reminders of Your Ex

When getting over a breakup, one of the first things you need to do is purge your home or apartment of all reminders of your ex.

"Sometimes humans want to lessen that man or woman off for a term which will heal. This ought to in all likelihood appear to be placing up employer barriers, doing away with them out of your social media, and making it smooth to friends and circle of relatives which you don't need to talk approximately them till you're prepared to speak approximately it," Pash notes.

If you're trying to find to drift on from a past dating, eliminating reminders of your ex can be a beneficial step inside the gadget. Here are some hints to take into account:

1. Declutter bodily gadgets: Go via your private home and gather any gifts, photos, or incredible possessions that remind you of your ex. Consider every storing the ones gadgets away or disposing of them inside the occasion that they no longer keep sentimental cost.

2. Unfollow on social media: Unfollow or unfriend your ex on social media structures to lessen the risk of seeing their posts and updates.

You also can don't forget taking a wreck from social media altogether for a while.

three. Remove pictures from your cellphone: Delete any snap shots or texts out of your smartphone that convey lower decrease again memories of your ex.

four. Avoid commonplace locations: If there are nice places that you companion with your ex, try to avoid them for a while.

This can offer you with some place to heal and technique your feelings.

5. Focus on self-care: Engage in sports activities that make you experience correct and will let you forget about approximately your ex.

This can be some thing from exercising to studying a excellent ebook, to spending time with buddies and own family.

Remember, shifting on takes time and all of us's adventure is one-of-a-type.

Be mild with your self and focus on what's high-quality for you and your emotional nicely-being.

Get Rid of or Store Physical Reminders

It is difficult to transport on and heal from a breakup in case you though have your ex's photograph at the nightstand or if you sleep of their vintage sweatshirt. It can be useful to get rid of reminders of them from your house.

Of direction, this does not advise you need to burn their property, throw their stuff into the street, or sell the entirety they gave you, but you want to as a minimum box those gadgets up.

If you have bodily reminders of past events or relationships that you would like to get rid of or hold, there are a few matters you may do to assist make the machine less tough:

1. Sort via your objects: Start with the aid of going via all the objects you need to cast off or shop, and kind them into piles based totally on their significance to you. This will allow you to make choices about what you need to keep and what you want to permit pass of.

2. Decide what to maintain: Consider each object and ask yourself whether or now not it holds sentimental fee, is useful, or holds realistic rate.

If an object might no longer in shape into such a lessons, it may be time to let it pass.

three. Store objects you want to maintain: If you've got got gadgets which you want to preserve, however do now not need to preserve out within the open, don't forget storing them in a subject or bin. Label the box or bin with a description of its contents so that you can without difficulty discover what you want in the future.

four. Donate or sell gadgets: If you have gadgets which may be however in outstanding state of affairs but now not hold personal value to you, hold in mind donating them to a charity or selling them.

5. Get rid of devices: For devices which is probably damaged or not useful, don't forget throwing them away or recycling them.

Remember, the motive is to maintain what is substantial to you and take away what now not serves a cause. The manner can be emotional, however it may also deliver a enjoy of closure and can help you flow into earlier.

Return some component that belongs to them if you want, or donate it to charity. The desire is yours.

But apprehend that having reminders of your ex which are with out issue to be had is going to hinder your development. So, do yourself a preference and at the least positioned it in storage.

If you have physical reminders that carry decrease again painful memories, it is able to be hard to allow circulate of them. However, retaining onto those gadgets also can save you you from shifting on and healing.

Here are a few recommendations that let you each dispose of or store bodily reminders in a manner that permits you to permit pass of the beyond and drift beforehand:

1. Decide what you need to preserve: Before you begin getting rid of bodily reminders, take the time to reflect on what gadgets are certainly huge to you and what devices are protecting you yet again.

2. Create a memory field: If you find it hard to component with bodily reminders, recall growing a memory box wherein you may keep objects that maintain sentimental rate. You can check the gadgets inside the field each time you enjoy discover it impossible to resist, however having them out of sight will let you circulate on.

3. Donate devices: If you have got got had been given gadgets which you no longer need or use, remember donating them to a neighborhood charity or someone in need. This assist you to experience proper approximately letting bypass of the physical reminder and may convey delight to someone else.

four. Repurpose gadgets: If you have were given bodily reminders that you can not part with however don't need to reveal, undergo in thoughts repurposing the object into something new. For example, you can flip a t-shirt from a past event into a cover or a piece of jewellery.

five. Seek help: If you're struggling with letting bypass of bodily reminders, take into account achieving out to a therapist or a help enterprise. They will will let you paintings through your feelings and make bigger a plan for letting skip.

Remember, letting pass of bodily reminders is a private system and what works for one character may not artwork for each different. Be kind to yourself and permit yourself to take some time you want to technique your emotions

Get Rid of Social Media and Digital Reminders

While you are at it, you moreover can also have to take away your ex from your social media money owed. Even even though you'll be curious about what they're up to, receiving consistent reminders through photos and posts will maintain you caught in the beyond. It furthermore may be painful too in case you see your ex with a new partner.

So, as difficult as it can be to do, unfriend and unfollow your ex as quickly as possible. You may furthermore even want to block them from seeing your posts and updates. The fewer connections you need to every distinctive the less difficult it is going to be to move

If you are seeking to restrict your publicity to social media and digital reminders, there are some steps you may take:

1. Limit the amount of time you spend on social media: Set strict closing dates for yourself for the way a whole lot time you spend on social media every day, and stick with them. You can also use equipment like Freedom or SelfControl to dam distracting web sites.

2. Turn off notifications: Go into your cellphone's settings and flip off notifications from social media apps. You can also do this for e-mail and different apps that deliver notifications. This will assist you keep away from the consistent pull of latest notifications

and will let you be greater aware about at the same time as you take a look at your phone.

three. Unfollow debts that make contributions to feelings of hysteria or negativity: Take a ruin from human beings or money owed that make you sense horrible or compelled out. You can also mute or unfollow money owed that continuously publish reminders or notifications.

4. Delete the apps: If you are actually having problem breaking your social media dependancy, endure in mind deleting the app in short. You can constantly down load it all over again later.

5. Seek possibility activities: Finally, discover possibility sports that bring you pleasure and rest. This ought to embody studying, writing, exercising, spending time with buddies and circle of relatives, or pursuing a hobby.

Chapter 8: Break The Bonds Of The Past

Breaking the bonds of the past can recommend various things to large people, but it normally refers to releasing oneself from awful reviews, emotions, ideals, and forms of behavior that can be retaining one decrease lower again from attaining their full ability or happiness. It can involve confronting and overcoming beyond traumas, forgiving oneself and others, letting bypass of grudges and resentments, and gaining knowledge of to stay in the present 2nd.

Breaking the bonds of the beyond isn't easy, and often calls for strive and resolution, but it may bring about more peace of thoughts, stepped forward relationships, and a more exciting existence. Some techniques to start breaking the bonds of the past consist of remedy, mindfulness practices, journaling, and spending time with supportive friends and family.

Breaking the bonds of the past can be a hard however worthwhile enjoy. It includes letting circulate of horrible reviews, worrying occasions, and horrible idea styles which have been defensive you lower again. Here are some approaches that will help you harm the bonds of the beyond:

1. Acknowledge your feelings and feelings: Acknowledge the ache and damage that you have professional in the past. Allow your self to revel in these emotions, rather than suppressing them.

2. Seek treatment: Therapy can be a brilliant manner to manner and heal from beyond traumas. A highbrow fitness expert allow you to paintings through the ones emotions and increase a plan to transport forward.

three. Practice self-care: Take care of your self bodily and emotionally with the useful resource of project sports activities that convey you pleasure and peace.

four. Surround yourself with notable people: Surrounding yourself with exquisite and supportive human beings will allow you to to revel in much less remoted and extra stimulated to art work via your past.

5. Let bypass of grudges: Holding onto anger and resentment closer to others can keep you trapped within the past. Try to forgive those who've harm you and permit pass of any grudges you'll be retaining.

Breaking the bonds of the beyond takes time, staying power, and strive, however with the right help and strategies, it's miles feasible to triumph over

One of the maximum effective "experience higher fast" techniques to triumph over emotional trauma or grief is known as "breaking the bonds of the past."

It stems from the belief that terrible emotions and behaviors are regularly based totally mostly on past memories which might be every poisonous or misinterpreted. This approach requires handiest five smooth steps.

write out the solutions to the subsequent questions:

1. When modified into the ultimate time you struggled, had the painful or disruptive memory or feeling, or felt struggling? Write down the information.

2. What have been you feeling on the time? Describe the main feeling.

three. When became the number one time you had that feeling? In your mind, bear in mind yourself on a educate going backward through time. Go once more to the time even as you first had the feeling. Write down the incident or incidents in element.

four. Can you bypass lower once more even in addition to a time at the same time as you had that precise feeling? Write down the information of the actual incident.

five. If you have got were given a smooth concept of the origins of the emotions, are you able to disconnect them by way of the use of reprocessing them through an adult or determine mind-set, or reframe them in mild of new facts? Consciously disconnect the emotional bridge to the past with the idea that what passed off in the beyond belongs in the beyond, and what takes location now may be what topics.

Here's an instance of the way this will work.

(3.2) How A Teen Learned To Leave The Past Behind

Nate, 15, came to look me at Amen Clinics due to the fact he have end up suffering from panic attacks. He had several episodes an afternoon at the identical time as he felt like he changed into choking or drowning. His respiration have emerge as shallow, speedy, and worked.

His coronary coronary heart raced, he broke out in a sweat, and he felt as even though he modified into loss of life. Nate hated the ones episodes, and the concern of having them have grow to be so overwhelming that he stopped going to highschool. During his 2d session with me, I went via the subsequent steps with him.

1. When changed into the closing time you had a panic assault?

Nate stated it turn out to be the day earlier than. He turned into ingesting dinner whilst all of a surprising, he felt like he have turn out to be starting to choke. He couldn't get air, his coronary coronary heart commenced to race, he emerge as sweating, and felt as even though he changed into going to die

.

2. What you've got been feeling on the time? Describe the principle feeling.

Nate said he felt as despite the fact that he have become going to die.

3. In your mind, take into account your self on a train going backward via time. Go lower decrease lower back to a time even as you first had the feeling which you were going to die.

The teen sat there for a minute after which started out to choke.

It regarded like he have become having a panic attack proper in the the the front of me. I requested him to respire slowly and tell me what changed into happening. He slowed his respiratory, wiped his forehead, and informed me about a time even as he turn out to be 6 years vintage.

He changed into sitting at a lunch desk at college and by accident swallowed a plastic wrapper from a sweet bar. He began out to choke on the wrapper. Initially, no person located him. He said he started to show blue. He couldn't breathe, and no one observed.

He notion he changed into going to die. After what appeared like an eternity, a teacher observed him and did the Heimlich maneuver on him, dislodging the wrapper. Nate stated he had forgotten approximately the event till now.

four. After he settled down and composed himself, I requested him to go decrease again even further in his mind to appearance if there has been an earlier time at the same time as he had the sensation he became going to die.

He closed his eyes and said he remembered a time even as he grow to be very more youthful. He changed into coming out of a totally dark region into a place packed with colourful lights, lights that felt heat. People have been transferring around. He felt worry. He couldn't breathe, and something lousy included his face. He felt as even though he have become going to die.

To my amazement, Nate had simply defined a transport revel in. When he opened his eyes, I asked him if he knew some factor approximately his shipping. He said no, no one had ever talked to him approximately it. I invited his mom to return once more into the room and asked her approximately his begin revel in.

She informed me that he turned into a meconium toddler, in which the infant's feces get into the amniotic fluid, which may be very risky for the contemporary infant. He modified into born blue and had to be resuscitated via the use of the scientific doctor. His mother said she had in no way mentioned it with Nate. She didn't want to worry him.

5. Break the bonds of the past thru an adult or determine mind-set or reframe them in slight of latest records.

With Nate's mother in the room, I took him decrease again to each of these instances. First, with the start enjoy, I had the grown teenage Nate bypass all over again and provide an explanation for to the toddler what had took place.

The infant modified into in problem for a fast time, however the doctors helped clean him up so he need to breathe typically. I then took him via the sweet wrapper incident and had the teenage Nate tell 6-yr-vintage Nate that he's thankful to the teacher who helped him and that he is alive, well, and wholesome (and he had to save you consuming candy wrappers).

After that session, Nate's panic assaults disappeared. I noticed him a few extra times, however basically disconnecting his gift signs and symptoms from the beyond sensitizing event took care of them.

Chapter 9: Definition Of Ptsd

Post-Traumatic Stress Disorder (PTSD) is a intellectual fitness state of affairs which can enlarge after experiencing or witnessing a demanding event. Traumatic sports activities can encompass natural screw ups, critical injuries, physical or sexual assault, conflict, or different violent memories.

PTSD is classified as a trauma and strain-associated sickness and is characterised via the usage of the re-experiencing of the worrying occasion thru flashbacks, nightmares, or intrusive thoughts. Individuals with PTSD may additionally avoid triggers associated with the demanding event, experience terrible modifications in temper and cognition, and showcase hyperarousal, which include being with out trouble startled or feeling constantly on guard.

Symptoms of PTSD can variety in severity and might effect someone's every day lifestyles, including their relationships, work, and favored properly-being. It is essential to attempting to find help and guide for recovery from PTSD, due to the fact the signs and symptoms and signs can get worse over the years and result in extraordinary mental health situations, which encompass despair and substance use problems.

The evaluation of PTSD requires meeting particular necessities stated within the Diagnostic and Statistical Manual of Mental Disorders, Fifth Edition (DSM-5). To be diagnosed with PTSD, an man or woman want to were uncovered to a worrying event, skilled symptoms and signs and signs and symptoms for greater than a month, and characteristic as a minimum one re-experiencing symptom, one avoidance symptom, terrible changes in temper and cognition signs and signs, and hyperarousal symptoms and symptoms and signs and symptoms and signs and symptoms.

It is vital to be aware that not anybody who opinions a disturbing event will expand PTSD. Some people may additionally enjoy acute stress illness, it in reality is a similar but shorter-lived circumstance that lasts among three days and one month after the traumatic occasion. However, if symptoms persist beyond one month, it could be indicative of PTSD.

In end, PTSD is a highbrow fitness situation that can enlarge after experiencing or witnessing a worrying event. Symptoms can effect a person's each day existence and may worsen over the years if left untreated. It is essential to trying to find assist and guide for recovery from PTSD to improve popular well-being and remarkable of existence.

Importance of Seeking Help for Recovery

Post-Traumatic Stress Disorder (PTSD) is a complicated and hard circumstance that may have a big effect on a person's existence. Symptoms of PTSD can variety in severity and might intrude with each day sports sports, relationships, and art work. Seeking help for PTSD restoration is important to enhance best of life and prevent signs from worsening.

One of the essential aspect motives to are searching for for assist for PTSD is to obtain an correct evaluation. PTSD is a complex situation that can present otherwise in every character. An accurate assessment is vital to developing an effective treatment plan that meets the character's unique desires. Seeking assist from a mental health expert, along with a psychologist or psychiatrist, can help ensure an correct analysis and the development of the proper treatment plan.

Another cause to are looking for help for PTSD is to accumulate treatment for signs and symptoms and signs and symptoms and signs and signs. There are severa powerful treatments to be had for PTSD, which embody psychotherapy, remedy, and complementary and opportunity remedies. Seeking assist from a intellectual health professional can assist people get right of get right of entry to to those treatments and achieve the aid they want to manipulate their signs and symptoms.

In addition to receiving treatment for signs, searching out help for PTSD can also provide emotional help. PTSD may be a lonely and putting aside enjoy, and searching out help from a highbrow health expert, assist group, or loved ones can offer a experience of connection and understanding. This emotional aid can assist humans revel in lots much less on my own of their recuperation adventure and offer a safe vicinity to particular their mind and feelings.

Another important cause to are looking for help for PTSD is to prevent the improvement of diverse intellectual health conditions. PTSD can increase the risk of growing wonderful highbrow fitness situations, including despair, anxiety, and substance use issues. Seeking assist for PTSD can provide people with the gear and manual had to manipulate symptoms and symptoms and save you the improvement of various intellectual fitness situations.

Finally, looking for help for PTSD can decorate general nicely-being and quality of lifestyles. PTSD need to have a profound effect on a person's life, and looking for help for recuperation can offer individuals with the belongings, help, and treatment needed to manage symptoms and signs and enhance their regular well-being.

In give up, on the lookout for help for PTSD restoration is crucial to enhance satisfactory of lifestyles, manipulate signs and symptoms, save you the development of different intellectual fitness conditions, and get hold of emotional guide. It is vital to are looking for assist from a intellectual health expert, guide organization, or loved ones to build up an correct diagnosis, get proper of entry to treatment, and collect the emotional manual had to manipulate symptoms and signs and enhance ordinary nicely-being.

Overview of the Book

This ebook is a comprehensive manual to overcoming Post-Traumatic Stress Disorder

(PTSD) and conducting restoration. The e-book is designed to offer human beings with an knowledge of PTSD, its causes, symptoms, and the unique treatment alternatives available to manage and triumph over the condition.

The ebook is split into nine chapters, with each monetary destroy focusing on a fantastic thing of PTSD recovery. Here is an outline of what you could assume to find out in every economic disaster:

Understanding PTSD

Post-Traumatic Stress Disorder (PTSD) is a mental health situation which could make bigger after experiencing or witnessing a annoying occasion. PTSD can have a excellent effect on someone's existence and may purpose signs and symptoms and symptoms that interfere with every day sports, relationships, and paintings. This bankruptcy will offer an in-intensity expertise of PTSD, which incorporates its reasons, symptoms, and varieties of trauma which can reason the state of affairs.

Causes of PTSD

PTSD can make bigger after publicity to a disturbing event. Traumatic occasions can encompass herbal failures, extreme accidents, physical or sexual assault, warfare, or different violent stories. PTSD also can boom after experiencing a existence-threatening infection or harm or witnessing a traumatic occasion taking location to someone else.

Symptoms of PTSD

PTSD signs and symptoms can range in severity and may be divided into four commands: re-experiencing, avoidance, horrible modifications in temper and cognition, and hyperarousal. Re-experiencing symptoms and symptoms can consist of flashbacks, nightmares, and intrusive mind. Avoidance signs and symptoms and signs can include fending off places, humans, or conditions that remind the individual of the demanding occasion. Negative changes in temper and cognition can encompass feeling numb, losing hobby in activities, and experiencing feelings of guilt or disgrace. Hyperarousal symptoms can consist of being with out issue startled, feeling continuously on shield, and experiencing anger or irritability.

Types of Trauma That Can Lead to PTSD

Any annoying event can potentially result in PTSD, however a few occasions are much more likely to motive PTSD than others. These embody:

Sexual attack or abuse

Combat or navy publicity

Physical attack or violence

Being in a crucial twist of fate or herbal catastrophe

Witnessing a stressful occasion happening to someone else, alongside facet a cherished one

It is critical to word that now not all of us who research a annoying event will amplify PTSD. The danger of developing PTSD can rely upon severa factors, such as the severity and duration of the disturbing occasion, the character's age and gender, and whether or not or no longer or no longer the individual has a history of highbrow health conditions or trauma.

In quit, PTSD is a highbrow health circumstance that can increase after experiencing or witnessing a disturbing occasion. Symptoms can range in severity and can intervene with day by day activities, relationships, and paintings. Traumatic sports which could result in PTSD can encompass sexual attack, fight publicity, bodily violence, injuries, herbal disasters, and witnessing worrying events going on to a person else. Understanding the reasons and signs and symptoms of PTSD is important to developing effective treatment and manipulate strategies.

Chapter 10: Causes And Risk Factors

Post-Traumatic Stress Disorder (PTSD) is a intellectual health situation that may develop after experiencing or witnessing a disturbing occasion. While publicity to a demanding occasion is a big danger detail for developing PTSD, there are different factors which could growth an man or woman's hazard of growing the situation. This bankruptcy will offer an in-intensity facts of the reasons and threat factors for PTSD.

Causes of PTSD

The primary cause of PTSD is exposure to a stressful occasion. Traumatic activities can consist of natural failures, extreme injuries, physical or sexual attack, battle, or different violent opinions. However, now not all of us who memories a worrying event will expand PTSD. The development of PTSD can depend on numerous factors, which include the severity and length of the worrying occasion, the individual's age and gender, and whether or not or now not or now not the man or woman has a data of intellectual health situations or trauma.

Risk Factors for PTSD

In addition to exposure to a demanding event, severa danger factors can increase an man or woman's threat of developing PTSD. These encompass:

Genetics

There can be a genetic component to the development of PTSD. Research has proven that genetic factors may also play a function in an character's danger of developing PTSD after publicity to trauma.

Brain Chemistry

Brain chemistry also can play a feature within the development of PTSD. Research has validated that humans with PTSD can also have imbalances in positive neurotransmitters, along with serotonin and norepinephrine.

Childhood Trauma

Individuals who have expert trauma inside the course of formative years, which include abuse or overlook, can be much more likely to expand PTSD later in life. Childhood trauma can effect the improvement of the thoughts and might increase an individual's vulnerability to developing highbrow health situations later in existence.

Lack of Social Support

Individuals who lack social help, such as friends and circle of relatives, can be much more likely to increase PTSD after experiencing a demanding occasion. Social help can provide a buffer in opposition to the bad results of trauma and might help individuals cope with pressure.

Other Mental Health Conditions

Individuals with special intellectual health situations, collectively with despair or anxiety, may be more likely to increase PTSD after experiencing a stressful occasion. These conditions may want to make it extra difficult to deal with pressure and can boom vulnerability to growing PTSD.

In surrender, PTSD is typically due to publicity to a demanding occasion, however numerous threat elements can growth an person's danger of developing the situation. These encompass genetics, mind chemistry, youth trauma, lack of social assist, and different mental fitness conditions. Understanding those motives and risk elements is essential to growing effective treatment and manipulate techniques for PTSD.

Symptoms and Diagnosis

Post-Traumatic Stress Disorder (PTSD) is a highbrow fitness state of affairs that might enlarge after experiencing or witnessing a worrying event. PTSD signs can variety in severity and can intervene with each day sports activities sports, relationships, and work. This bankruptcy will offer an in-intensity understanding of the symptoms and signs and symptoms of PTSD and the way of diagnosing the condition.

Symptoms of PTSD

PTSD signs and symptoms and signs and symptoms and signs may be divided into 4 categories:

Re-experiencing

Re-experiencing symptoms can encompass flashbacks, nightmares, and intrusive mind. Individuals with PTSD may also experience excessive or extended misery at the same time as reminded of the worrying event.

Avoidance

Avoidance signs can encompass averting places, people, or situations that remind the person of the demanding event. Individuals with PTSD can also additionally keep away from talking or considering the stressful occasion.

Negative Changes in Mood and Cognition

Negative changes in temper and cognition can encompass feeling numb, losing hobby in sports, and experiencing feelings of guilt or shame. Individuals with PTSD may have hassle remembering key components of the traumatic occasion.

Hyperarousal

Hyperarousal symptoms and symptoms and symptoms can embody being with out issues startled, feeling constantly on guard, and experiencing anger or irritability. Individuals with PTSD might also moreover additionally have hassle napping or concentrating.

Diagnosing PTSD

The diagnosis of PTSD calls for meeting unique criteria stated inside the Diagnostic and Statistical Manual of Mental Disorders, Fifth Edition (DSM-5). To be identified with PTSD, an character want to have been uncovered to a demanding event, professional signs and symptoms and signs and symptoms for additonal than a month, and have at least one re-experiencing symptom, one avoidance symptom, horrible modifications in temper and cognition signs and signs, and hyperarousal symptoms and symptoms.

The way of diagnosing PTSD typically includes a comprehensive assessment via manner of a intellectual health professional, consisting of a psychologist or psychiatrist. The evaluation can also moreover encompass a overview of the individual's scientific statistics, a talk in their signs and symptoms, and a mental evaluation.

It is crucial to observe that diagnosing PTSD may be difficult, as signs and signs and signs and symptoms can be much like the ones of different highbrow fitness conditions. It is essential to gather an correct evaluation to growth an effective treatment plan.

In quit, PTSD symptoms may be divided into 4 training: re-experiencing, avoidance, horrific changes in temper and cognition, and hyperarousal. The evaluation of PTSD calls for meeting particular necessities referred to within the DSM-five and usually includes a complete assessment with the useful resource of a highbrow health expert. Understanding the signs and symptoms and signs and diagnostic technique of PTSD is vital to developing effective remedy and control strategies for the situation.

Types of Trauma That Can Lead to PTSD

Post-Traumatic Stress Disorder (PTSD) is a highbrow fitness state of affairs that might increase after experiencing or witnessing a demanding event. Traumatic activities can vary in severity and might effect human beings in specific techniques. This monetary ruin will offer an in-intensity knowledge of the first-rate varieties of trauma that would result in PTSD.

Sexual Assault or Abuse

Sexual attack or abuse is a worrying event that may bring about the development of PTSD. Sexual assault can embody rape, molestation, or any undesirable sexual contact. Sexual abuse can consist of any form of sexual hobby that an man or woman did not consent to.

Combat or Military Exposure

Combat or navy exposure can be a annoying event that may cause the improvement of PTSD. Military employees who've experienced combat publicity, together with being in a war area or witnessing violence, may be liable to growing PTSD.

Physical Assault or Violence

Physical assault or violence may be a disturbing occasion that would bring about the improvement of PTSD. Physical assault can include domestic violence, attack thru a stranger, or a few different form of physical violence.

Accidents or Natural Disasters

Accidents or natural failures can be a traumatic occasion which could motive the development of PTSD. Examples can embody automobile accidents, earthquakes, hurricanes, and fires.

Witnessing Traumatic Events Happening to Others

Witnessing worrying activities taking region to others, collectively with a loved one, additionally can be a disturbing occasion which can purpose the development of PTSD. Examples can embody witnessing a violent crime, experiencing the sudden loss of life of a cherished one, or witnessing a natural catastrophe.

It is crucial to examine that no longer virtually every person who tales a demanding event will boom PTSD. The development of PTSD can depend on several factors, which embody the severity and length of the annoying occasion, the individual's age and gender, and whether or not or no longer the individual has a records of intellectual fitness conditions or trauma.

In end, PTSD can boom after publicity to a annoying occasion. Traumatic events which can result in PTSD can encompass sexual attack or abuse, combat or army exposure, physical assault or violence, injuries or herbal failures, and witnessing disturbing occasions going on to others. Understanding the sorts of trauma which can reason PTSD is crucial to figuring out human beings vulnerable to developing the circumstance and developing powerful remedy and control strategies.

Conventional Treatments for PTSD

Post-Traumatic Stress Disorder (PTSD) is a intellectual health condition which can increase after experiencing or witnessing a worrying occasion. While PTSD may be a difficult condition to govern, numerous conventional treatments are to be had that could assist individuals manage signs and signs and symptoms and benefit restoration. This monetary catastrophe will offer an in-intensity records of traditional remedies for PTSD.

Medication

Several drug treatments may be prescribed to govern symptoms and signs and symptoms and signs and symptoms of PTSD, such as antidepressants, anti-tension medicinal drugs, and antipsychotic medicines. These capsules can help manage symptoms inclusive of hysteria, melancholy, and sleep disturbances. However, remedy by myself isn't always usually enough to reap recuperation from PTSD, and is regularly implemented in mixture with exceptional remedies.

Psychotherapy

Psychotherapy is a type of speak treatment that can be effective in coping with signs and symptoms and signs and symptoms of PTSD. Cognitive-behavioral remedy (CBT) is one form of psychotherapy this is normally used to deal with PTSD. CBT involves working with a therapist to pick out and undertaking terrible idea patterns that would make a contribution to PTSD signs and signs and symptoms and symptoms. Other kinds of psychotherapy, which encompass exposure remedy, can help people confront and manner annoying sports in a secure and managed surroundings.

Eye Movement Desensitization and Reprocessing (EMDR)

EMDR is a form of therapy that includes focusing on a worrying occasion while project a guided eye motion workout. This therapy can assist people approach demanding reminiscences and reduce the effect of PTSD signs and symptoms.

Group Therapy

Group treatment includes taking component in treatment with a set of people who have professional comparable traumatic occasions. Group remedy can offer social manual and might assist people experience plenty less isolated in their recovery adventure.

Family Therapy

Family therapy includes operating with a therapist to beautify verbal exchange and remedy conflicts internal a family. Family treatment can help enhance own family relationships and help humans of their recuperation from PTSD.

It is crucial to be conscious that each man or woman's experience with PTSD is specific, and remedy plans want to be tailored to satisfy the individual's precise wishes. Conventional remedies for PTSD may be powerful, however no longer all treatments will artwork for anybody. It can be crucial to attempt severa precise treatments or a aggregate of treatments in advance than locating what works amazing for the individual.

In stop, conventional remedies for PTSD can encompass remedy, psychotherapy, EMDR, commercial enterprise agency therapy, and circle of relatives therapy. Each remedy has its personal advantages and barriers, and remedy plans want to be tailor-made to fulfill the man or woman's precise dreams. It is essential to art work with a highbrow health professional to boom an powerful remedy plan and acquire recuperation from PTSD.

Chapter 11: Medications

Post-Traumatic Stress Disorder (PTSD) is a intellectual fitness condition that could enlarge after experiencing or witnessing a annoying occasion. Medications may be prescribed to control signs and symptoms of PTSD, which include antidepressants, anti-anxiety drug remedies, and antipsychotic medicinal pills. This financial disaster will offer an in-depth know-how of medicines commonly used to treat PTSD.

Antidepressants

Antidepressants are a form of medicinal drug usually used to treat symptoms and signs and symptoms of depression and anxiety related to PTSD. Selective serotonin reuptake inhibitors (SSRIs) and serotonin-norepinephrine reuptake inhibitors (SNRIs) are normally used to treat PTSD. These drugs paintings with the aid of developing the tiers of top notch neurotransmitters in the thoughts, which could decorate mood and decrease symptoms and signs of hysteria.

Examples of antidepressants generally used to deal with PTSD embody sertraline, fluoxetine, and venlafaxine.

Anti-Anxiety Medications

Anti-anxiety medicinal tablets, which incorporates benzodiazepines, may be prescribed to govern signs and symptoms of hysteria related to PTSD. These medicinal drugs artwork through improving the effects of a neurotransmitter referred to as gamma-aminobutyric acid (GABA), which can reduce tension. However, benzodiazepines can be addictive and may cause drowsiness and impaired coordination, so they may be normally prescribed for brief-time period use. Examples of anti-tension medicinal pills normally used to cope with PTSD encompass alprazolam and clonazepam.

Antipsychotic Medications

Antipsychotic pills may be prescribed to control signs of paranoia or psychosis associated with PTSD. These drug treatments artwork with the resource of blockading the consequences of dopamine, a neurotransmitter that would contribute to psychotic signs and symptoms and symptoms. Examples of antipsychotic medicinal pills commonly used to treat PTSD embody risperidone and quetiapine.

It is important to be aware that medicinal pills on my own are not usually enough to achieve recuperation from PTSD, and are frequently used in aggregate with other treatments, such as psychotherapy or EMDR. Medications can have facet outcomes, and it's miles critical to artwork with a healthcare company to apprehend the risks and advantages of each treatment.

In end, medicinal capsules may be prescribed to manipulate signs and symptoms and signs of PTSD, along aspect antidepressants, anti-tension drugs, and antipsychotic medicines. These drug treatments can be powerful in managing signs and signs and symptoms and signs and signs collectively with tension, despair, and sleep disturbances related to PTSD. However, drug treatments are generally applied in mixture with exceptional remedies, and it's far important to artwork with a healthcare company to enlarge an effective remedy plan for PTSD.

Psychotherapy

Post-Traumatic Stress Disorder (PTSD) is a intellectual fitness situation that might expand after experiencing or witnessing a stressful occasion. Psychotherapy, additionally known as speak therapy, is a form of treatment that may be effective in managing signs of PTSD. This financial ruin will offer an in-intensity understanding of psychotherapy commonly used to address PTSD.

Cognitive-Behavioral Therapy (CBT)

Cognitive-behavioral treatment (CBT) is a shape of psychotherapy normally used to cope with PTSD. CBT includes strolling with a therapist to emerge as aware about terrible concept styles that could contribute to PTSD signs and signs and signs and symptoms. The therapist will assist the individual to challenge these poor thoughts and growth greater first-rate and adaptive techniques of questioning. This remedy also can encompass publicity remedy, which involves confronting and processing disturbing memories in a steady and controlled surroundings.

Eye Movement Desensitization and Reprocessing (EMDR)

Eye Movement Desensitization and Reprocessing (EMDR) is a form of remedy that involves focusing on a disturbing event on the equal time as challenge a guided eye movement exercising. This treatment can help humans system stressful reminiscences and decrease the impact of PTSD signs and symptoms.

Prolonged Exposure Therapy (PE)

Prolonged Exposure Therapy (PE) includes confronting and processing annoying reminiscences in a secure and managed surroundings. The character will art work with a therapist to regularly reveal themselves to the demanding memory or state of affairs that triggers their PTSD signs and symptoms and signs and symptoms, at the same time as studying coping talents to manipulate their anxiety.

Group Therapy

Group remedy includes taking component in remedy with a set of people who've skilled comparable traumatic activities. Group remedy can provide social manual and can help people experience a lot less remoted of their healing adventure. This remedy can be mainly effective for human beings who have expert trauma in a set placing, together with navy employees or survivors of natural screw ups.

Family Therapy

Family remedy involves running with a therapist to beautify communication and resolve conflicts within a own family. Family treatment can help decorate own family relationships and useful resource human beings in their recuperation from PTSD.

It is important to word that every individual's experience with PTSD is precise, and remedy plans have to be tailored to fulfill the character's specific wishes. Psychotherapy may be an effective remedy for PTSD, but now not all types of treatment will artwork for every man or woman. It can be crucial to attempt severa one-of-a-type remedies or a mixture of treatment options earlier than locating what works splendid for the man or woman.

In conclusion, psychotherapy is a kind of treatment that may be powerful in coping with signs and signs of PTSD. Commonly used kinds of psychotherapy for PTSD encompass cognitive-behavioral remedy, EMDR, prolonged exposure treatment, enterprise treatment, and own family treatment. Understanding the only-of-a-type styles of psychotherapy to be had is essential to growing an effective remedy plan for PTSD.

Eye Movement Desensitization and Reprocessing (EMDR)

Post-Traumatic Stress Disorder (PTSD) is a intellectual fitness situation that could growth after experiencing or witnessing a traumatic occasion. Eye Movement Desensitization and Reprocessing (EMDR) is a type of treatment that may be powerful in handling signs and symptoms and signs and symptoms of PTSD. This bankruptcy will offer an in-intensity know-how of EMDR.

What is EMDR?

EMDR is a form of remedy that includes focusing on a worrying occasion whilst carrying out a guided eye movement exercise. The eye moves implemented in EMDR can encompass monitoring the therapist's finger, paying attention to tones achieved in alternating ears, or the usage of a light bar that actions back and forth. The cause of

EMDR is to assist individuals machine demanding recollections and reduce the impact of PTSD signs and symptoms and symptoms.

How does EMDR paintings?

EMDR is primarily based on the idea that annoying reminiscences can turn out to be stuck inside the thoughts, and that this could make contributions to the development of PTSD. The eye moves utilized in EMDR are notion to imitate the speedy eye movements that stand up all through the fast eye motion (REM) section of sleep, that is while the mind strategies reminiscences. The eye moves utilized in EMDR are believed to assist the mind device annoying recollections and reduce the emotional impact of these recollections.

What does an EMDR consultation seem like?

EMDR instructions normally start with the therapist accumulating facts approximately the individual's facts and identifying disturbing recollections which can be contributing to PTSD signs and signs and symptoms. The therapist will then guide the individual thru a series of eye actions at the equal time as focusing on the worrying reminiscence. The eye moves are generally repeated numerous instances while the individual focuses on the demanding memory.

As the man or woman progresses through EMDR periods, the intensity of the stressful memory and related emotions need to lower. The aim of EMDR is to help the person way traumatic reminiscences and reduce the emotional impact of these reminiscences.

Is EMDR powerful?

Research has shown that EMDR may be an effective remedy for PTSD. EMDR has been decided to be as effective as specific forms of psychotherapy, which includes cognitive-behavioral treatment, in reducing signs and symptoms of PTSD. EMDR has furthermore been placed to be powerful in treating one of a kind highbrow health situations, on the side of tension and melancholy.

It is important to be conscious that EMDR won't paintings for everybody, and that now not all therapists are educated in EMDR. It is vital to artwork with a therapist who's knowledgeable and professional in EMDR to make sure the extremely good feasible very last outcomes.

In cease, EMDR is a shape of therapy that can be effective in dealing with symptoms of PTSD. EMDR consists of specializing in a traumatic occasion at the same time as challenge a guided eye movement exercise. The eye moves utilized in EMDR are believed to assist the thoughts manner demanding reminiscences and decrease the emotional impact of these reminiscences. EMDR has been decided to be an effective treatment for PTSD, however no longer everybody can also moreover reply to this form of treatment. Working with a professional and expert therapist is essential to ensure the great feasible final results with EMDR.

Complementary and Alternative Therapies for PTSD

Post-Traumatic Stress Disorder (PTSD) is a intellectual health situation that could expand after experiencing or witnessing a worrying occasion. While conventional treatments, which encompass remedy and psychotherapy, may be effective in coping with signs and symptoms of PTSD, some human beings may also moreover select out to discover complementary and possibility treatments. This financial ruin will provide an in-intensity knowledge of complementary and opportunity treatment plans for PTSD.

Mindfulness-Based Therapies

Mindfulness-primarily based treatments, which include mindfulness-based totally totally stress discount (MBSR) and mindfulness-primarily based completely absolutely cognitive treatment (MBCT), can be powerful in dealing with signs of PTSD. These remedies involve analyzing to recognition on the existing 2nd and developing an interest of thoughts and emotions with out judgment. Mindfulness-based remedy alternatives can assist people manage symptoms of hysteria and melancholy associated with PTSD.

Yoga

Yoga can be effective in dealing with signs and symptoms of PTSD, such as tension and sleep disturbances. Yoga includes practicing bodily postures, respiratory sporting sports, and meditation. Yoga can assist humans decorate their physical and highbrow fitness, lessen strain, and enhance their everyday well-being.

Acupuncture

Acupuncture includes the insertion of skinny needles into unique factors at the body. Acupuncture can be powerful in coping with signs of PTSD, together with tension, despair, and sleep disturbances. Acupuncture is thought to assist regulate the body's strength go with the glide and sell restoration.

Art Therapy

Art treatment includes the use of innovative expression, along with drawing or portray, to help individuals manner demanding sports and manage signs and symptoms and symptoms and signs of PTSD. Art remedy can provide a secure and nonverbal way for people to specific emotions and paintings through worrying memories.

Animal-Assisted Therapy

Animal-assisted therapy includes interacting with animals, which incorporates puppies or horses, to beautify highbrow fitness and nicely-being. Animal-assisted remedy can be effective in dealing with symptoms of PTSD, at the side of anxiety and depression. Interacting with animals can offer a sense of comfort and help, and can help humans experience more associated with the arena spherical them.

It is critical to be aware that complementary and opportunity restoration procedures should be applied in mixture with traditional remedies, collectively with treatment and psychotherapy, and now not alternatively for those treatments. It is also crucial to paintings with a healthcare agency to make sure that those recovery methods are constant and suitable for the individual.

In cease, complementary and opportunity recovery procedures can be effective in dealing with signs and symptoms of PTSD. Mindfulness-based absolutely treatments, yoga, acupuncture, art work treatment, and animal-assisted remedy can provide people with greater equipment to manipulate signs and symptoms and signs and symptoms and decorate their preferred properly-being. It is essential to use those remedies in aggregate with traditional treatments and to artwork with a healthcare company to make certain that those remedies are strong and suitable.

Chapter 12: Mindfulness And Meditation

Post-Traumatic Stress Disorder (PTSD) is a intellectual fitness state of affairs that might expand after experiencing or witnessing a worrying occasion. Mindfulness and meditation are strategies that may be effective in dealing with symptoms and symptoms of PTSD. This monetary disaster will provide an in-depth records of mindfulness and meditation.

What is mindfulness?

Mindfulness is the exercising of specializing within the prevailing second and becoming aware about mind, emotions, and bodily sensations with out judgment. Mindfulness includes being absolutely present within the 2nd and accepting the experience with out trying to find to alternate it. Mindfulness can assist people manipulate signs and symptoms of hysteria and melancholy related to PTSD.

What is meditation?

Meditation is the practice of schooling the thoughts to popularity and attain a rustic of calm and relaxation. Meditation can encompass focusing at the breath, a mantra, or a visualization. Meditation can help individuals control signs of anxiety and despair related to PTSD, and may decorate normal properly-being.

Mindfulness-Based Stress Reduction (MBSR)

Mindfulness-Based Stress Reduction (MBSR) is a shape of remedy that consists of reading mindfulness strategies to govern pressure and beautify ordinary well-being. MBSR may be effective in coping with signs and signs and symptoms of PTSD, consisting of anxiety and despair. MBSR includes practicing mindfulness strategies, together with meditation and yoga, to enhance intellectual and bodily health.

Mindfulness-Based Cognitive Therapy (MBCT)

Mindfulness-Based Cognitive Therapy (MBCT) is a form of treatment that includes combining mindfulness techniques with cognitive-behavioral treatment (CBT). MBCT can be powerful in handling symptoms and signs and symptoms of PTSD, which includes tension and melancholy. MBCT consists of reading mindfulness strategies to control bad concept patterns which can make a contribution to PTSD symptoms.

Benefits of mindfulness and meditation

Mindfulness and meditation can provide people with severa blessings, which includes:

Reducing signs and symptoms of hysteria and depression

Improving ordinary nicely-being

Reducing strain

Improving sleep

Improving cognitive characteristic

Reducing signs and symptoms and signs and symptoms of chronic ache

It is vital to be aware that mindfulness and meditation must be applied in combination with traditional treatments, which includes treatment and psychotherapy, and now not alternatively for these remedies. It is likewise critical to art work with a healthcare company to ensure that the ones strategies are secure and suitable for the individual.

In conclusion, mindfulness and meditation can be powerful strategies in managing signs and signs and symptoms and symptoms of PTSD. Mindfulness includes that specialize inside the winning second and becoming privy to mind, emotions, and bodily sensations without judgment. Meditation includes schooling the thoughts to advantage a kingdom of calm and relaxation. Mindfulness-Based Stress Reduction (MBSR) and Mindfulness-Based Cognitive Therapy (MBCT) are forms of remedy that use mindfulness strategies to manage symptoms of PTSD. Mindfulness and meditation can offer severa advantages, however need for use in aggregate with traditional remedies and under the guidance of a healthcare employer.

Yoga

Post-Traumatic Stress Disorder (PTSD) is a intellectual fitness situation which could enlarge after experiencing or witnessing a stressful event. Yoga is a workout that may be effective in dealing with symptoms of PTSD. This economic catastrophe will provide an in-intensity data of yoga.

What is yoga?

Yoga is a exercising that includes physical postures, breathing bodily video games, and meditation. The bodily postures, or asanas, are designed to beautify flexibility, strength, and balance. The respiration bodily games, or pranayama, are designed to enhance respiratory and decrease stress. The meditation, or dhyana, is designed to enhance highbrow attention and benefit a kingdom of calm and rest.

How can yoga help with PTSD?

Yoga can be effective in dealing with signs of PTSD, collectively with anxiety and sleep disturbances. Yoga includes physical postures, respiratory carrying sports activities, and meditation, which can assist people manage pressure, lessen tension, and enhance sleep. Yoga also can assist human beings decorate their physical and highbrow nicely-being, that may make contributions to essential healing from PTSD.

Types of yoga

There are numerous forms of yoga that may be effective in dealing with signs and symptoms and signs and symptoms of PTSD, together with:

Hatha yoga: This is a slight form of yoga that entails critical postures and respiration carrying activities.

Vinyasa yoga: This is a extra active form of yoga that involves flowing from one pose to the following on the same time as coordinating motion with breath.

Restorative yoga: This is a moderate form of yoga that includes defensive poses for numerous mins on the equal time as the use of props, at the side of blankets and blocks, to guide the frame.

Kundalini yoga: This is a kind of yoga that includes repetitive actions and breath artwork to enhance power float and mental reputation.

Benefits of yoga

Yoga can provide human beings with severa blessings, which consist of:

Reducing signs and symptoms of tension and melancholy

Improving preferred well-being

Reducing pressure

Improving sleep

Improving cognitive characteristic

Reducing symptoms and symptoms of persistent pain

It is critical to observe that yoga should be implemented in combination with conventional treatments, which incorporates remedy and psychotherapy, and not as a possibility for those remedies. It is likewise essential to paintings with a healthcare issuer to ensure that yoga is strong and appropriate for the character.

In give up, yoga is a exercise that may be powerful in dealing with signs and symptoms of PTSD. Yoga consists of physical postures, respiratory bodily video video games, and meditation, which could assist human beings manage strain, reduce anxiety, and enhance sleep. There are numerous sorts of yoga that may be powerful in handling signs and symptoms and signs and symptoms of PTSD, and yoga can provide numerous benefits, inclusive of lowering signs and symptoms and symptoms of anxiety and depression, improving commonplace properly-being, and lowering strain. Yoga ought to be carried out in mixture with conventional treatments and below the steering of a healthcare enterprise.

Acupuncture

Post-Traumatic Stress Disorder (PTSD) is a highbrow health situation that may increase after experiencing or witnessing a demanding occasion. Acupuncture is a shape of treatment that may be effective in handling symptoms of PTSD. This financial ruin will offer an in-depth facts of acupuncture.

What is acupuncture?

Acupuncture consists of the insertion of skinny needles into particular elements on the body. Acupuncture is based on the concept that the frame's electricity glide, or Qi, can grow to be blocked or imbalanced, important to physical and intellectual health issues. Acupuncture is notion to help alter the body's energy go with the go with the flow and sell recovery.

How can acupuncture assist with PTSD?

Acupuncture can be powerful in dealing with signs and symptoms and signs and symptoms of PTSD, along side tension, melancholy, and sleep disturbances. Acupuncture can help humans manage signs thru selling rest, lowering pressure, and improving sleep. Acupuncture can also help human beings beautify their normal properly-being, that would make a contribution to regular recuperation from PTSD.

What does an acupuncture consultation appear like?

Acupuncture lessons normally begin with the acupuncturist collecting facts about the man or woman's medical facts and identifying precise symptoms or problems. The acupuncturist will then insert thin needles into unique points on the frame. The needles are generally left in vicinity for numerous mins, for the duration of which technology the individual also can revel in a experience of warmth or tingling.

Is acupuncture secure?

Acupuncture is generally taken into consideration steady whilst carried out with the resource of a licensed and certified acupuncturist. It is crucial to work with a certified acupuncturist to make certain that the needles are inserted nicely and that the treatment is suitable for the person.

Benefits of acupuncture

Acupuncture can offer human beings with numerous benefits, which include:

Reducing signs of anxiety and melancholy

Improving regular nicely-being

Reducing stress

Improving sleep

Reducing signs and symptoms and signs and symptoms and symptoms and signs of chronic pain

It is critical to take a look at that acupuncture want to be utilized in mixture with traditional treatments, together with remedy and psychotherapy, and no longer as a opportunity for those remedies. It is also essential to paintings with a healthcare organisation to make certain that acupuncture is stable and appropriate for the individual.

In give up, acupuncture is a form of treatment that may be effective in coping with symptoms and symptoms of PTSD. Acupuncture includes the insertion of thin needles into unique factors at the body, and is believed to assist adjust the body's energy waft and sell recuperation. Acupuncture can provide severa blessings, which incorporates reducing signs and symptoms of tension and melancholy, improving normal well-being, and lowering pressure. Acupuncture ought to be utilized in combination with conventional treatments and under the steerage of a healthcare provider.

www.ingramcontent.com/pod-product-compliance
Lightning Source LLC
Chambersburg PA
CBHW051727020426
42333CB00014B/1198